# Rambling Memories of a World War II Fighter Pilot

*Hope you enjoy the book*

*Doug McLaughlin*

**Doug McLaughlin**

Bloomington, IN  Milton Keynes, UK

*AuthorHouse™*
*1663 Liberty Drive, Suite 200*
*Bloomington, IN 47403*
*www.authorhouse.com*
*Phone: 1-800-839-8640*

*AuthorHouse™ UK Ltd.*
*500 Avebury Boulevard*
*Central Milton Keynes, MK9 2BE*
*www.authorhouse.co.uk*
*Phone: 08001974150*

© 2006 Doug McLaughlin. All rights reserved.

No part of this book may be reproduced, stored in a retrieval system, or transmitted by any means without the written permission of the author.

First published by AuthorHouse 8/10/2006

ISBN: 1-4259-2016-0 (sc)

Library of Congress Control Number: 2006905967

Printed in the United States of America
Bloomington, Indiana

This book is printed on acid-free paper.

# Dedication

My wife has been a tremendous help in writing this book in so many ways. Probably the most important was that she edited the entire book for grammatical errors. She also has been a tremendous help by showing me better ways of expressing myself, along with being a big morale booster.

# Why I Wrote This Book

I really wrote this book because of what happened when I was talking to four young guys at a friend's party. They seemed to be fascinated to hear about my World War II combat experiences. They kept urging me, for instance, to tell them more about when I, as a Naval fighter pilot in the Pacific, joined up on four Jap fighters, an event I describe later in the book. They sat so mesmerized listening that as I wound up the story I couldn't help stretching the truth a bit by telling them I made too steep a dive at the end of the encounter, went into the drink and drowned. Up to that last part they were sitting on the edge of their seats, hanging on every word. Then, as they realized I was only pulling their legs with the part at the end, they wanted to hear more stories. It got me thinking that maybe my wartime yarns might also be of interest to others, considering the growing interest in the "World's Greatest Generation" and World War II. Hence this book

# Acknowledgement

I would like to refer readers to "Wings of Gold" by Gerald Astor. This is an excellent book on the entire U.S. Naval Air Campaign in World War II. On many occasions where I could not remember certain events, I was helped immensely by this book.

I would also like to thank my friend and computer genius, Jim Hack of Network Plus, for all his help in putting this book together.

Also, kudos to my sister, Betty MacCoon, for her painstaking proofreading.

## Contents

**CHAPTER 1**
Starting At The Beginning ................................................. 1

**CHAPTER 2**
Back To Those High School Days Again ........................... 9

**CHAPTER 3**
The War Years Begin ...................................................... 15

**CHAPTER 4**
Getting Up In The Air ..................................................... 18

**CHAPTER 5**
Training Antics ............................................................... 21

**CHAPTER 6**
In The Service At Last .................................................... 25

**CHAPTER 7**
The War Yarns Begin ..................................................... 27

**CHAPTER 8**
Things Get Better ........................................................... 32

**CHAPTER 9**
More War Yarns ............................................................. 35

**CHAPTER 10**
The Task Force .............................................................. 38

**CHAPTER 11**
Training Time ................................................................ 41

## CHAPTER 12
Decision-making Time ...................................................... 46

## CHAPTER 13
Back To Training ............................................................... 48

## CHAPTER 14
The Ensign Gold Bar At Last ............................................ 53

## CHAPTER 15
The Real Thing .................................................................. 59

## CHAPTER 16
The Fun Times ................................................................... 67

## CHAPTER 17
Finally, The Combat Zone ................................................. 73

## CHAPTER 18
Palau–Where I Almost Bought It ...................................... 82

## CHAPTER 19
The Ulithi Storm ................................................................ 90

## CHAPTER 20
The Marianas Turkey Shoot .............................................. 94

## CHAPTER 21
Flight Into Darkness .......................................................... 97

## CHAPTER 22
Survival Stories ................................................................ 102

## CHAPTER 23
The Fight Goes On ........................................................... 104

**CHAPTER 24**
How It's Done ............................................................. 108

**CHAPTER 25**
A Day In The Life Of A Pilot .................................... 111

**CHAPTER 26**
Close Encounter Of The Wrong Kind ...................... 121

**CHAPTER 27**
Getting Back To The Ship ......................................... 125

**CHAPTER 28**
More Engagements ..................................................... 131

**CHAPTER 29**
Goosed! ...................................................................... 136

**CHAPTER 30**
Combat Air Patrol ..................................................... 138

**CHAPTER 31**
The One That Got Away ........................................... 140

**CHAPTER 32**
Forgotten Action ........................................................ 142

**CHAPTER 33**
Heading Home ........................................................... 143

**CHAPTER 34**
Stateside & Training A New Combat Team ............. 147

**CHAPTER 35**
My Dream Fighter Plane ........................................... 153

CHAPTER 36
    The End Of The War ............................................................. 159

CHAPTER 37
    Post-war Times ...................................................................... 162

CHAPTER 38
    Space Rockets ........................................................................ 166

CHAPTER 39
    Coming Down To Earth ........................................................ 170

CHAPTER 40
    Back To The Sea-Going Navy .............................................. 174

CHAPTER 41
    China Watch .......................................................................... 180

CHAPTER 42
    Home Again .......................................................................... 187

CHAPTER 43
    Anti Submarine Warfare And Korea .................................... 190

CHAPTER 44
    Taps ....................................................................................... 193

# Prologue

There's a saying that there are old pilots and bold pilots, but no old, bold pilots. I guess I'm not bold because I sure am old—you decide.

Another popular belief is that your whole life passes before your eyes when you think you are about to die. That's so much baloney. When I sat strapped in my Grumman fighter plane, the F6F-3 Hellcat, on the suddenly deserted deck of an aircraft carrier in the mid-Pacific in 1944, with machine gun bullets thudding all around me from two Japanese dive-bombers, I didn't experience a thing.

I was kind of surprised I didn't get scared because it is usually when you are under attack and have no control over the situation that the fear comes. It was really over too soon to get scared. Maybe it is because your training kicks in causing your mind to concentrate on the job at hand. What with shoulder straps holding me tight against my seat and everybody diving over the side onto the catwalks along the side of the ship there really wasn't anything I could do about it anyway.

# CHAPTER 1
## STARTING AT THE BEGINNING

If I had remembered my life, it would have gone something like this, with a jump start to the beginning of our country's participation in WWII.

It was December 7th 1941, and for those who lived then it was a time we would never forget. I can still see so vividly my buddies and myself standing around my Model A Ford with a rumble seat, in front of my folks' home in Beverly Hills California, our home town. We had just heard of the Japanese attack on Pearl Harbor and we wondered what was going to happen next. We were about 21 years of age and in the prime of our young lives--hard to picture us like that now. But hey. We were young, all full of ideas of what we were going to do in life and oh yes, we kept an eye out for a well turned ankle. In our day, that's about all we got to see. It is funny I don't feel any different now at some 84 years of age, except for being wiser, I hope, than when I was 21. Also, physically I'm not quite as able as I was at that younger age, currently not quite ready to enter the Olympics.

In a way our town was different than most towns because there were some movie actors and actresses in our high school although my buddies and I weren't any different from other small-town boys. I can remember some celebrities like Betty White, the TV star who was for a while in my class in elementary school. Later because she was smarter she was advanced to a higher grade and still later she was discovered by Hollywood and became a star. I remember that she made quite an impression on the boys in our sixth-grade class, so much so that several of them went down alleys picking flowers from back yards in the rain and presented them to her. I thought she was kind of cute but at eleven I wasn't into girls just yet. If I remember right, later while at Beverly Hills High School, she was selected as the best-looking girl in the senior class.

A lot of us young guys in high school went out for sports like track and football, just like today. I chose football although I would have been better off in track because I wasn't big enough. I can still remember running a couple of laps around the track and beating the rest of the runners in a freshman class race pretty badly. But instead I chose to go out for the 'B' football team as an end. I think I was on about the 4th string team. We were like cannon fodder for the third, second and first-string teams and many an afternoon I came home sore and beat up.

Later in the season I did get to go to the Rose Bowl to play another high school's 'B' team and after we ran the score up to something like 40 to 0 the coach put me in. I was so excited I was off-side about 3 times and the opposing player thought I was nuts. The following year, I grew too big for the 'B' team and I can't remember why I didn't go on to junior varsity, probably because at about 130 pounds I still just wasn't big enough.

I remember, when they weren't going to a studio school, you'd see actors like Mickey Rooney and Jackie Coogan getting out of a chauffeured limousine parked in front of the high school. The rest of us didn't pay much attention to them as we walked or rode our bicycles to school.

Mickey Rooney had his own football team and he would play with selected, talented players on his team against put-together teams of local youth, at a park called La Cienega

Park. Take a wild guess who won those games. While Rhonda Fleming went to Beverly Hills High School too, she was several years behind us.

I know I'm leaving out others from our high school who became famous, but I want to dispel any image that life was any different for my buddies and me because the small town we lived in was Beverly Hills. We were typical teenage boys from low to middle-income bracket families. By the way I earned that Model A I mentioned earlier by delivering newspapers and later by delivering Western Union telegrams.

There were of course wealthy families in Beverly Hills but they lived in another part of the city. I remember delivering a telegram once at Christmas to one of these mansions and seeing a brand new convertible in the driveway all tied up in red ribbon.

I was fortunate because I grew up with this close bunch of five or six fellows who went around together everywhere most of the time. We were healthy young guys, except for one or two, and we all ended up volunteering for service in the armed forces. One of my buddies, Earl Nelson, had some kind of stomach disorder that classified him as 4F. This was the designation that exempted one from military service. There were others that had physical disorders like my friend "Fatty Mitch" who had a disfigured arm that kept him out of the service.

Of course we did get into mischief occasionally, like the time five of us climbed over the fence at the city reservoir, and stood on the bank and tried to see who could pee the farthest. My friend Earl won because he had an unusually high arc, earning him the title of "winner-over-all."

Arthur Marx, whose father was Groucho Marx, was a star on our high school tennis team and my buddy Mike Zimmerman was a teammate of his. Mike, who is now 85 years of age, still plays tennis every day. Maybe that's what keeps him healthy. Today, there are only the two of us left from that bunch of guys who ran around together. Funny—none of them died in the war. But they say we are dying off at the rate of 1500 a day although probably more than that by now.

After the war I met guys like my neighbor here in Washington, Dave Webber, a great guy and not just because he favored the Navy Air Corps over the Army Air Corps. He was turned down by the Navy Air Corps because he was color blind. I never understood that because during all my flying days I can recall only one time when my not having or having color blindness would have had anything to do with my flying an airplane. The airfield tower blinks a red or green light indicating cleared to take off or not to, but that could be overcome by memorizing when they were flashed. Anyway he went over to the U.S. Army Air Corps (which after the war became the Air Force), stayed in line behind a lot of other guys until he had the charts memorized, and was accepted. Later he flew over Germany on a bunch of bombing raids--so much for color blindness. Like so many from that era he has died, too.

Another buddy, Freddy Edwards, went into the Army Air Corps and served as an enlisted man. I remember him telling me that the officers made the enlisted men stand in the rain to watch a movie in New Guinea when there were plenty of seats available in the sheltered officer's section. He wasn't very fond of officers. After the war he inherited his grandfather's huge, earth-moving business, becoming an instant multi-millionaire. Officers from his old service group would come around to see him looking for a job and he turned them all down flat, loving every minute of it. It doesn't pay to treat those under you badly as it may come back to haunt you someday. Anyway like so many others Freddy is gone too.

Another close buddy, Gilbert Harris, joined the Army Air Corps and was assigned to pilot gliders. These gliders were loaded with troops and then released over France in the big Normandy invasion. Gilbert survived the war but died about 10 years ago from throat cancer.

I'll always remember Gilbert's father. He was a lawyer and he belonged to literally every club that featured drinking. One of those clubs was called, if I remember correctly, "The L.A. Marching and Chowder Society." The club's sole function seemed to be to get together and drink booze. Gilbert's dad was also a very funny guy. When my wife and I got married he was in the audience of the church making loud whispered remarks because the minister forgot to tell everybody to sit down after my bride reached the altar, causing everybody to stand during the whole ceremony. Also, there was a large lady in front of him with a huge hat and although Gilbert's dad was a big man he couldn't see over this woman's hat. I could hear Mr. Harris's loud whispers griping about that woman's hat even as far away as where I stood by the altar. My wife's family had decided that there would be no booze at the reception and good old Mr. Harris didn't let that go by without a few choice remarks, either. He was one of my favorite dads.

When the minister asked "Do you promise to love, honor and obey?" I thought that was just for my bride. Boy was I ever wrong. I turned out to be the one obeying.

My best man, Bob Grant, was an aircraft gunner in the Army Air Corps and saw action in air raids in Italy and thereabouts. He died pretty early in life from a diving accident off Monterey, California. When I joined the Navy my folks had a farewell party for me and invited all my buddies. I remember a trick we pulled on old Bob. He was a little on the short side, about 5"7 or so, and very self-conscious about it. He was always rocking on his tiptoes when he talked to you. All the rest of us were taller than him except Freddy. When my sister took a group picture of us that day, we managed to get Freddy up on something to make him seem much taller than Bob. I don't think Bob ever really forgave me for that.

I was the second one to go into the service, since Mike Zimmerman went into the Marine Corps right out of high school. Mike has a funny way of walking, it's kind of like the way a duck walks, and he took one heck of a ribbing in the Marine boot camp from the drill inspectors.

# CHAPTER 2
## BACK TO THOSE HIGH SCHOOL DAYS AGAIN

Those were fun days, with lots of going to the beach on weekends. I would talk my dad into letting me drive his car to the beach and we'd all pile into it. I charged each one of my buddies for gas telling them my dad charged me. Years later they found out this wasn't true and they never let me forget it.

It's funny that we weren't much into girl chasing in those days. I only went out twice with any girls while I was in high school. The first time was when my folks, sister and I went over to Catalina on the big white steamer. I met a girl on the ship and spent some time with her on the ship with, of course, my younger sister hanging over the back of the seat on the ship bugging us.

I went out with this girl a couple of times later on until she sent me a "Dear John" letter. My friend Rodney and I took the letter out in my backyard, painted red ink on the back of the letter and then took my .22-caliber rifle and shot a hole in the letter so that the red color showed on the back. Rodney wrote on the letter that I had shot myself over her "Dear John" letter and was in a bad way. She got such a kick out of it she relented about going out with me again, but by then I wasn't very interested anyway and that relationship died.

The other date was with a very pretty girl in high school and I can still remember her name, Ethel Tobin. We went out on a date after we had to settle the fact that we would be going in my car, not her dad's chauffeur-driven limo. She was a nice girl as well as pretty, helping her dad raise her younger siblings because her mother had died, and she really impressed me, but then when I called her back I really botched it up good. She said she had another engagement but said she wanted to go out again some time. My ego couldn't tolerate being turned down and I didn't follow up.

I don't think any of my buddies even went to a school prom. I know I never did. We were just a bunch of kids in a world about to go to war, though we didn't know it. We spent most of our time going to the beach for body surfing and swimming. There used to be a gambling ship anchored just over 3 miles off the Santa Monica beach and I remember having made a small duck boat out of canvas and wooden stringers and rowing out to the ship to watch it from the water while the high rollers lost their money.

We also were really interested in hiking in the Sierra Nevada Mountains and even the Hollywood Hills. There was an old hermit who lived up in the Hollywood hills and we would hike up to see him. Sometimes he would tell us some scary or other kinds of stories. He was a harmless old galoot.

Later when we were older we made our own backpacks with a large canvass bag and wood strips that we steamed into curved pieces and put together into a shape to carry the bag. Then in the summer time Rodney Sprigg and I would drive up to Yosemite and hike in the backcountry. I had always loved the great outdoors, either in the mountains or near water, and never cared for cities. I would have loved to have grown up in a small town in Oregon or Washington because they are in the Alpine region of the world with evergreen trees everywhere and such wonderful clear, fresh air. To hear the wind whispering through the trees and smell the pines and other trees was what appealed to me.

Doug McLaughlin

We started going up to Yosemite National Park after going on a trip with the Boy Scouts up into the Sierra Nevada Mountains one summer. Rodney and I felt that they hiked too slowly and Rodney, being something of maverick, didn't like all the rules and regulations so we decided in the future we would go by ourselves. It didn't help that with the Boy Scout troop there were several non-rugged kids that slowed us down when hiking. I remember one fat kid who was very gassy, so bad we had to put him in the rear of the troop to escape the fumes. This kid could have been a secret weapon for the army.

I wore out a couple of pairs of boots hiking in the backcountry of Yosemite clear up into the higher areas of California's Sierra Nevada Mountains, including the Mt. Lyle Glacier. On one of the trips, while about 4,000 feet above the Yosemite Valley, Rodney and I decided we were getting a bit ripe so we jumped into the Merced River which was right along the trail that went from the floor of Yosemite Valley up to Tuolumne Meadow. The river came down from the High Sierras, which were at 10,000 on up to 14, 000 feet. That water was like jumping into ice water so we started to jump back out when all of a sudden along the trail this troop of Girl Scouts comes slowly moving along on horseback. Since we were in the nude we had to hunker down in that freezing water till they rode by. Wow. Was it ever cold. I can almost still feel it.

On the same hiking trip as the one above, only now we were way up in the High Sierras and isolated from other hikers, we encountered a problem. A large black bear got interested in us and started following us. We were carrying a large chunk of cheese that we would slice for lunch along the way. We also had a side of salt pork that we would slice into strips for bacon in the morning. I don't know which one it was that the bear wanted but he was very persistent.

We kept throwing rocks at him during the day and would chase him off, but at night it was a different thing. He would try to get at our knapsack of food every night. First we tried tying the knapsack to a small tree and he just kept shaking the tree until we woke up and chased him off. Then we put it on the ground with pots and pans around it and when he tried for it he woke us up, banging the pans as he roared through the campsite.

Rodney got the bright idea that he would tie one end of a piece of rope to his wrist and the other end to the knapsack with the food. Along about midnight I heard loud yelling, waking me up just in time to see Rodney go sailing out of his sleeping bag bare-ass naked (we slept that way). The bear had just come rambling through our campsite, grabbed the knapsack and headed off dragging Rodney with him. Eventually Rod got loose, but here we were many miles from anywhere (and in 1936 or '37 there were nowhere near the number of hikers there are today) so there was no one to get food from either. We took off after that bear and we could trail him because there was no top to the knapsack and all that food was spilling out. You have to picture two naked, shoeless boys in pitch black chasing a bear with flashlights and yelping as we stepped on sharp rocks and sticks. We eventually got back the knapsack and most of the food but never got the cheese slab, or was it the side of pork that the bear kept.

A couple more pre-war incidents: One Halloween we put some burning film in the elevator of the Beverly Wilshire Hotel, a very prestigious hotel. If you have ever smelled burning film you will know why cops were soon looking for us everywhere.

Another time a bunch of us got thrown in jail because Bob Grant started a fight with some other young guys when he sicced his dog on a dog belonging to one of the other kids. Freddy Edwards escaped the cops and then went to the jail to plead for the rest to be released and he got thrown in with us. We were just a bunch of normal boys with no idea we would soon be heading off to war.

# CHAPTER 3

## THE WAR YEARS BEGIN

Prior to the war, there had been reports in the papers about friction between Japan and the United States. What it seem to boil down to was the Japanese were claiming we were cutting off their supply of scrap metal, oil and other materials that they used in their war machine in the conquest of China and elsewhere. We were opposed to their war activities, particularly in the attacks on China. It looked like war was really coming. However the Japanese had sent a couple of envoys who were in Washington, D.C. to discuss how to solve these problems so when the attack on Pearl Harbor came it was a really sneaky thing to have done and a big surprise to us, particularly when you considered Japan had their envoys in Washington, D. C. solely to discuss better relationships between the two countries.

At our age our thoughts were elsewhere until that historic December 7 morning. As President Roosevelt said, "It was a day that will live in infamy". Oddly enough the Japanese, to this day, do not seem willing to recognize it was they who committed this foul deed and they also have forgotten about some of their other atrocities like the notorious "Rape Of Nanking, China," where more people died than in Nagasaki and Hiroshima combined. There were other atrocities like the 'Bataan Death March" and the torture of prisoners.

It was very soon after the attack on Pearl Harbor that almost all of us were in the service and many of us were shortly after that on our way to combat zones. This was a different era; everybody, once we were attacked, was behind the war effort. The recruiting offices for the services had lines of men running around the block. Even those who didn't qualify for the armed services contributed in whatever way they could. It was totally different from the attitude today.

You who are reading this may never have heard of "Rosie the Riveter". These were the gals who worked in the aircraft factories and shipyards taking the places of men who had gone off to war. Other folks who were too old or for one reason or another didn't qualify to enter the various services contributed in whatever way they could. Gas rationing, sugar rationing, blackout wardens on patrol, scrap-metal drives, housewives saving bacon fat to be used in making ammunition; everybody helped.

# CHAPTER 4

## GETTING UP IN THE AIR

I had been attending the University of Southern California. Maybe you've heard of the school. Its football team, the Trojans, has been the national champion in college football for the last two years in a row. (I had to throw that in, to bug my UCLA and Notre Dame buddies.) Anyway, one of my courses was a government-sponsored flight training course C.P.T., Civilian Pilot Training. It was a program some far-seeing politician got established in colleges throughout the country to train pilots for the war he saw coming.

I had completed the basic, cross-country and advanced courses and acquired about 250 hours of solo flight time. I had started out flying a little single-engine plane called the Porterfield, similar to a Piper Cub. I flew it out of a little grass field southeast of Los Angeles, the Gardena airport. My first instructor was a woman, which was unusual then. While I sometimes complain about women drivers (particularly my wife's driving) I have to admit that lady flight instructor was a good teacher. I still remember when she told me I was ready to solo, after my completing some six to eight hours of flying dual. I lined the plane up in the grass field and shoved the throttle forward. The grass was so tall I was hoping I would have enough power to get airborne, but it was a piece of cake. I went around several times practicing touch-and-go landings until she was satisfied I wasn't going to kill myself.

Next were a number of solo flights that I remember with a fondness, mostly because I would dive down and in and around those big old cumulous clouds. In all of my flying days those were some of the most enjoyable times I had in the air. Going out to a small airfield at a little town and flying off into clear blue skies with some puffy white clouds and diving down on them, what more could you ask of flying?

Following the completion of the primary flying course at U.S.C., I entered the secondary program, also through U.S.C., where I received ground school training in navigation and other subjects to qualify for my private flying license. In secondary we had moved up to a two-seater bi-plane, the Waco, and learned acrobatics, night flying and other skills.

Before the war I had spent time in Oregon and used to go out to small fields and rent a small plane. I would take off and go fly around the clouds on a weekend and it was great fun. Those days, there were nowhere near the rules, regulations and, most of all, the crowds of airplanes in the air that there are today. Those were wonderful days.

As a matter of fact one of the reasons I decided I wanted to learn to fly was because I went up in a small plane with my buddy Rodney as pilot. At the end of the flight he put the plane in a steep tailspin toward the ground, pulling out just before he would have hit. It scared me so much I decided I had to learn how to fly too.

When the war broke out the whole program was moved to Douglas, Arizona. I remember taxing up in the Waco to a parking spot after a flight, with a silk neckerchief streaming out behind me and helmet and goggles. I can still see us getting out of the planes and walking behind a fence that bordered the airplane parking area with lots of young ladies ogling us through the wire fence. It was a romantic era and we took advantage of it.

# CHAPTER 5

## Training Antics

In Arizona we made many cross-country flights over the desert to various checkpoints to hone our flying skills. There was one incident in particular during a night-training flight, where we swooped down low along a railroad track toward an oncoming locomotive with our landing lights on. It was supposed to look like another train coming head-on to the train engineer, and I do think it did a pretty good job of scaring the poor guy.

I also remember we hedge-hopped all over the country on the navigation flights, scaring a few cows and sometimes incurring the wrath of our instructors as well as quite a few ranchers. Hedge-hopping is where you fly the plane really close to the ground, so close that sometimes you might come back with parts of bushes and tree branches in the wheels or maybe the bottom of the wings. It gives you a high, at least it did me, but this is not recommended, as there are all kind of rules against it, and of course it can be very dangerous. Later when flying Navy fighters while shore based, on more than one occasion I came back with tree branches or bushes hanging to the bottom of the wings. But I hope nobody tries this unless you are bent on committing suicide, or at the very least, losing your flying license.

After completing the third course after primary, secondary and cross-country I tried to enlist in both the Army Air Corps and the Navy Air Corps. However, there was a problem preventing me from getting into the military service as a flyer. I had only been a U.S. citizen for 8 years, having been born in Canada, and the services required 10 years. When I was 18 or so, before the U.S. got into the war, I had tried to enlist in both the Royal Canadian Air Force (RCAF) and the Eagle Squadron. I can't remember what went wrong with the Eagle Squadron but with the RCAF I drove up to Canada in my old Model A. On the way up there one of the cylinders blew out a piston in the San Francisco area. When I found out how much it cost to repair I just told the mechanic to put the head back on and disengage that piston. Needless to say while I drove on the highways with little loss of power the U.S. Army could have used me for a secret weapon from all the smoke I put out. I was also buying oil by the buckets.

When I finally got up to Canada I went to the RCAF in Vancouver to enlist. However, my dad had got wind of what I was doing through my Canadian uncle, who I had got in touch with since I had run out of money. I don't remember all that happened but somehow because Canada didn't want to ruffle relations with the good ole U.S.A., since they were receiving so much goods and materials and military equipment from us, and my dad I guess put pressure on them to keep me from joining, they asked me not to join the Canadian forces.

This started another episode in my life in driving back home. I got a job in a bakery, Gresham Bakery in Gresham, Oregon. I drove a bakery wagon in and around the farm communities below Mt. Hood. I would stop at a farm or ranch and sell them bread, doughnuts, and other goods. The farmers' daughters found out I was single young guy and they would always walk out to the bakery wagon and give me the google eyes.

I acquired a dog and we slept over the bakery. On my routes, I would stop for lunch and have all the blackberries I could pick along with a quart of milk from the milk truck when it drove by, along with several maple bars or doughnuts. I bloomed up to about 200 lbs from my normal weight of around 140. Eventually I drove back home, alarming the whole West Coast along the way with the black smoke my buggy poured out. On the way home I tried to get into the air arm of our military at several bases, still with no luck because of the 10-year citizenship requirement for both Army and Navy Air Forces.

# CHAPTER 6

## IN THE SERVICE AT LAST

I had become a citizen by derivation when my Canadian-born dad was naturalized and I was around 13 years old, which only added up to my having been a U.S. citizen for 8 years when the U.S. finally entered the war. Luckily for me, one day my dad met Wayne Morris, a then well known movie actor, at a Rotary Club meeting. Morris was now a recruiting officer for the Navy. He told my dad it would be no problem to get a waiver of the citizenship problem so I could enlist in the Navy Air Corps.

After completing all the tests I was sworn into the Navy Air Corps Cadet flight program by Wayne Morris. (Incidentally, he later became a Navy fighter pilot and shot down several planes, qualifying him as an "ace" which is five planes or more. An interesting sidelight, when Wayne Morris died, at a rather young age, his old fighter squadron held a big party up at the Naval Air Station Alameda with money he had left in his will for this purpose. I heard it was one heck of a wild party that lasted a couple of days).

My dad, being a doctor, arranged for my physicals, including the Wasserman test which was needed to qualify and which I flunked because the lab got the tests mixed up with someone else's. For any who don't know, the Wasserman test is to determine if you have any sexually transmitted diseases. Before it got squared away, I had to tell my dad my whole sex life, which was not much, in an attempt to get to the bottom of my problem. (My dad didn't think it was much, either.) I could have shot that lab technician.

# CHAPTER 7
## THE WAR YARNS BEGIN

Now we flash forward to January 1946, the war is over, and I am sitting in a separation center being separated from the Navy, when two high school classmates who hadn't made it into combat came up to me and wanted to hear about some of my combat experiences and Japanese planes I had shot down. I found it a bit ironic that these two, both former big shots on campus, were without headlines, whereas a relative nobody like me in high school had some small amount of newspaper notice for ships I had sunk and the planes I shot down. So I told them about the time I joined up on four Jap Zeros near Iwo Jima, where incidentally, I believed I was the first American plane to fly over the island. I will describe these incidents later.

Those two former classmates and I had been Navy fighter pilots in that era of "the world's greatest generation". The other two had completed training but hadn't made it into combat whereas I had because I had gone in sooner. My squadron flew off the USS Cabot, hull #28, a CVL (Light Cruiser Converted Aircraft Carrier). This class of carrier is still generally looked back upon as the toughest class to land on because the beam was so narrow and it was the second shortest carrier in length, next to the jeep carrier. You had better be lined up right, especially at night. While the F4U Corsair and the Grumman F4F also flew off Navy carriers during the war, the Navy's F6F Hellcat was the predominant fighter plane and it was the one I flew. It also had the highest number of kills in the Pacific of any aircraft, Army or Navy. Its kill ratio was 19 to 1. It was a very stable plane and able to absorb lots of punishment from the enemy as well as being an excellent plane for carrier landings. It was slower than the Corsair but faster than the Jap Zeros as well as faster than the F4F Wildcat. It was a Grumman-built plane, one in a long line of stable and solid planes with the Pratt and Whitney R2800 radial 2,000 horsepower engine. By using water injection you could acquire up to 100-or was it 200-more horsepower?

**The Grumman F6F Hellcat fighter with me as pilot.**

I should mention no military fighter plane was as maneuverable as the Jap Zeros; so if you got in a dog fight with one all they had to do was turn inside you and they would be on your tail and "goodbye you." Best to make runs on the enemy's planes getting on their tails, for "goodbye them." Of course there were exceptions when due to the inexperience of the Japanese pilot or on occasion when both planes are traveling at a high rate of speed the American plane might be able to turn inside the Japanese plane. I'm not sure but I think I read somewhere that the Zero was a copy of one of Howard Hughes' aircraft designs.

I learned later that General Claire Chenault of Flying Tigers fame cautioned against dog fighting in a P-40 with the Zero. This didn't only apply to the P-40 but to all other fighter planes around at that time as well. This is not to say that some pilots who did dog fight with the Jap planes couldn't or didn't win because many did on occasion but it was best to remember the inside turning capability advantage of the Japanese fighters.

As I said, if you tried to dog fight with a Zero, watch out, for the Jap planes could turn inside you and get on your tail. However, we held one enormous advantage, in that F6Fs had an armor plate behind the pilot's seat and self-sealing fuel tanks, and the Japs did not have either of these important safety features for their pilots. Our F6Fs could take a great deal more punishment than the enemy and we were faster.

When you shot at the Jap planes and hit them they would frequently explode or burn quickly, whereas the Hellcat normally would not unless it had been fired on for a while, most likely thanks to these two safety features. There were numerous stories of our F6F fighters making it back to the carriers all shot up with holes even in the engines.

At the very beginning of the war the fighter plane on carriers and the same one used by Marine pilots on the ground in the South Pacific was the F4F, called the Wildcat. It was much slower than both the Zeros and the Hellcat. So in the early days of the war when all we had in Navy and

Marine fighters was the F4F our pilots had both speed and maneuverability disadvantage when in combat with the Zeros. The battle of Midway and the air battles by the Marine pilots over Guadalcanal were good examples. I take my hat off to those Navy and Marine pilots who helped win those battles. Pilots like Butch O'Hare who died fighting to save his carrier, yet shot down so many Japanese fighters under such odds that he won the Congressional Medal of Honor. I believe he was credited with five or six planes shot down in one engagement. Marine fighter pilots like Joe Foss, Pappy Boyington and others did the same from land. In those days they frequently went up to intercept far more enemy planes than their forces had, and in an inferior airplane.

# CHAPTER 8

## THINGS GET BETTER

With the advent of the F4U Corsair (that's the plane with the kind-of inverted wings) and its 400-plus miles per hour maximum speed, which was mostly flown by Marine pilots off South Pacific Islands like Guadalcanal, the pendulum began to swing in our favor. There were also a few flown by Navy pilots off carriers. Add to that when the F6F replaced the little Grumman F4F with its superior speed and bigger guns in the wings (50 calibers) on the carriers, it pitted them at 380-plus top speeds against the Zero at about only 320 top speeds, finally giving our pilots an advantage. Incidentally, when I mention speeds that is when the plane is in a level position. In a dive you will develop much higher speeds.

*Rambling Memories*

***Cabot's Island in museum and me looking at it in 2004. The small Japanese flags represent Japanese planes that were shot down and the ships represent ships sunk by VF31, my Squadron and VT31.***

Getting back to my own combat plane, the F6F Hellcat, the island on the carrier and part of the wooden flight deck of the USS Cabot and her fighter squadrons, VF 31, my squadron, and the succeeding one, VF29, are featured in the Navy Air Museum in Pensacola, Florida, or were, prior to recent horrific hurricanes in and around Pensacola which I am told did a lot of damage to the Air Station and the museum. Painted on the island were the rows of Japanese flags for planes shot down and symbols of ships sunk that earned the Cabot the title of one of the most-decorated ships in the Navy.

There was another interesting display at the museum before the hurricanes, that may still be there. On the second floor they had decorated rooms with a lot of scenes from the 1940s such as barber shops, grocery and drug stores, and cars and trucks, with pictures and dummies of men, women and children in clothes of that era. It really took me back.

# CHAPTER 9

## MORE WAR YARNS

War has been described as hours of monotony punctuated with short periods of sheer terror. I won't ever forget that time I'm sitting in the cockpit of an F6F Hellcat on the catapult on the bow of the Cabot during the "Marianas Turkey Shoot", waiting to be launched. The "Marianas Turkey Shoot" was the name given to the clash of Japanese and American Navy fighter planes off Saipan, Tinian and Guam Islands in the Pacific in 1944. It was one of the turning points in the war in the Pacific, since some 300 to 400 Jap planes were reported to have been shot down in this combat engagement.

Getting back to my predicament on the catapult. This was the incident I mentioned earlier when the two Japanese planes decided to dive bomb my ship. Try to picture everybody on the deck of the carrier diving for cover. Mostly they dove into the cargo nets along side the deck of the carrier, or was it the catwalks along side the landing deck of the ship. The Japs, like us, when in a dive or glide bombing run, sprayed the target with machine gun fire. They used 20 mm cannons in the wings. Ours were 50 caliber machine guns. I'm not certain how many they had but we had six in the F6s' wings. Anyway, shells were hitting the, in those days, wooden deck, all around me, making this thumping noise. Later aircraft carriers were built with metal decks. Needless to say the signalman who directed me onto the catapult and the catapult officer who gave the signal to launch me had wisely dived for cover. So I was sitting in the plane's cockpit with the engine revving up waiting to be launched, all by my lonesome.

I am pretty well strapped in so there was no way I could get out of the plane in time before the dive bombers finished their run. How do I describe it when you are the target and no way of shooting back. Incidents like this are measured in seconds not minutes; I'll take that any day to slugging it out on the ground like the marines and soldiers. I take my hat off to those guys. But back to the cockpit where I was all tied in by my shoulder harness and seat belt, I just sat frozen hoping that the Jap pilot's aims were lousy or maybe they were shooting at some other part of the ship. The 20mm cannon shells hit the ship but their bombs did not, thank goodness. When I looked up they looked like they were passing through 5-10,000 feet above at somewhere around 350-plus knots and looked more like fighters than dive bombers and in my mind I can still see them to this day.

As soon as the enemy planes pulled out of their dives and speeded forward the catapult officer launched me. When airborne I retracted my wheels, then my flaps, and pushed everything to the firewall. The enemies by this time, due to their speed from the dive, were way ahead of the ship and flying through that murderous AA fire that our ships could bring to bear. Naturally, following them I ran through some of it too. Then, just as I was beginning to catch them and line up to down at least one of them, the ship's AA fire shot them both down, leaving me one disappointed pilot.

# CHAPTER 10

## THE TASK FORCE

A number of Navy fighting ships firing at mostly the same targets can be the most heavily concentrated firepower known to man. Maybe now I should describe what our task force looked like. It was called task Force 38 or 58 depending on which Admiral was in charge and sometimes called the Third or Fifth fleet. Try to picture somewhere around 12 to 15 destroyers in a huge circle. Then follow this with two to four cruisers, two battleships and two to four carriers all positioned in the center of this circle. I could be slightly wrong about the number of ships since I am going back some 60 years ago. But this is only one unit and might be called 58.1, 58.2, 58.3 or 58.4. Since there were four of these task forces, it was probably the largest armada of fighting ships ever assembled. When the

Admirals changed, the name changed to 38.1 from 58.1 and vice versa.

The Normandy invasion may have been larger in number of ships but many were troop transports and landing craft, and nowhere near as many men-of-war. I remember when we were on our way to Iwo on a surprise raid and the fleet was spread out as far as you could see, when our strictly maintained radio silence was broken by some Air Force pilot from one of the neighboring islands we had attacked and neutralized, He hollered out "J---- C----- look at all the ships!" I suppose I shouldn't complain; at least he didn't call them boats. (For those who don't know, boats are defined as craft which are, or can be, carried aboard ships. Ships cannot be carried this way.) Anyway, there were ships of war as far as the eye could see in any direction. To the Japanese pilots it must have been awesome.

Of course it wasn't like this in the beginning of the war. As a matter of fact in the beginning, it was exactly the opposite. The Japanese had a huge advantage over us in number of ships. Their battleships were bigger than ours with 17-inch guns as opposed to ours at 16 inches. They had almost twice as many carriers in their fleet as we had in ours and the carriers were even larger than ours then.

Before I go any further, I should mention I was no big hero or even close to one. As a matter of fact I only shot down three planes getting credit for one and a fraction because in one battle apparently my gun cameras didn't work. You see all kills are supposed to be confirmed by another pilot or the gun cameras. I don't even remember how many ships I sank. I think it was somewhere between four to six, more on that later. Of course I dropped a whole lot of bombs, usually 500 lb. ones, on shore installations or other ships and usually in a glide-bombing run, which is around a 60-degree angle and in these low altitude bombing runs there is usually plenty of AA fire.

I am really writing this rambling collection of experiences because some people, especially young guys, when they find out I was a WWII combat pilot, ask for stories and seem to be mesmerized when I tell some of them . I hope you as a reader will also enjoy them. I suppose my greatest claim to fame was that I shot down a "Tony" that was shooting down our leading ace and he confirmed it. I'll come to this later.

There were some incidents other than action scenes that were kind of typical of the times and a reader might find interesting or humorous--so read on.

# CHAPTER 11
## TRAINING TIME

To go back to the beginning, I went into the Navy Air Corps around the first of February or March 1942, shortly after Pearl Harbor. At that time I had an advantage with my 250 solo flight hours and training in acrobatics, cross-country flying, dead-reckoning-navigation-type flying and other valuable experience. This helped me go through the Navy E-Base (Elimination Base) qualifications at Long Beach and Los Alamitos Naval Air Station with ease.

One sidelight: The base was still under construction when I was at Long Beach so we roomed in boarding houses in town with almost no supervision for a month or so. This means we got away with murder and seldom made it back at night for what would normally have been bed-check time, because there was no bed check, and we spent our nights drinking beer and chasing girls. When the base at Los Alamitos was completed we moved into barracks and that was the end of our civilian-style life. Even then there were always a few who snuck out at night and came sneaking back to the base again after hours (never me, of course).

At Los Al we flew a biplane called the N3N which was made by the Navy, which was the reason for that designation. It was a kind of a fun plane, open cockpit and all. We learned acrobatics and basic stuff. Having had civilian training previously it was a piece of cake for me, particularly because the N3N was so similar to the Waco we flew in the civilian program—similar size and shape, both biplanes, with a like engine and weight of the airplane about the same.

Los Al was what was called an elimination base because the cadets were put through all kinds of physical drills designed to toughen them and eliminate the weaker ones, and those who couldn't get the drift of flying quickly enough were washed out. The tough physical part of training was true later on but not when I went through except for a minimal amount of training. The reason for that was in the early days of the war we lost a lot of pilots at Midway and other crucial battles and pilots were desperately needed, so we were almost rushed through training. U.S. Navy Torpedo Squadron 8 was completely wiped out in their attacks on the Japanese fleet at Midway, the sole survivor being an Ensign named Gay, who was shot down, floated around watching the battle from the water, and lived to become an Admiral. The U.S. losses were mostly due to flying an old outmoded torpedo plane, the TBD, because it was too slow. Also their torpedoes were very unreliable, not exploding on contact.

But at Los Al we cadets were still having some fun times, such as when the entire group of navy air cadets went to Long Beach for a Miss California pageant that was taking place. Another cadet and I escorted the winner on the stage, and boy was she a beauty. I tried to get a date but she wouldn't give me the time of day. The other cadet didn't even try. An officer told us later they had picked the two best-looking cadets to escort her. I had no idea I was good-looking. Anyway I guess I wasn't good-looking enough because I flunked out with her.

Another time I visited my buddy Gilbert Harris who was an Army Air Corps cadet at a base in Orange County, California. Our navy blue uniform made us look like officers, especially as there was a star on it--forgotten where. So when I visited Gilbert, the other Army Air cadets thought I was an officer. As a result they were saluting me right and left, since any officer from any arm of service outranks any cadet. Of course this bugged the heck out of Gilbert and he spent most of the time yelling at his comrades "He's only a cadet like us, quit saluting him!"

Recently my sister told me about one little comment made by my mother that you might enjoy. When we graduated from Los Alamitos, the Naval Air Station held a ceremony in which all the cadets marched on the tarmac passing in review in front of the Air Station brass, saluting as they passed. Friends and relatives were invited and they sat in the stands watching the ceremony. My mother spotted me marching with the rest and said "Oh look there goes Douglas and he is the only one in step all the others are out of step". I had been out the night before celebrating and was a bit hungover. So much for a mother's love.

After we graduated from Los Al we were shipped to Corpus Christi Naval Air Base and into our next stages of training. I had grown up in Southern California which is fairly low in humidity, so when we arrived in Corpus Christi and got off the train into that hot, humid weather it was quite a shock. It seemed to take awhile to get used to. I never did get used to the bugs, especially the mosquitoes. Every so often a plane would come over the barracks and spray the base with DDT and we prayed for those days, especially since it was summer and the mosquitoes were out in droves. Later this was shown to be harmful to the environment. I'm told that lately some scientists claim deaths from mosquito-borne malaria far outstripped the harm to the environment. I'll leave that to the experts. Anyway to us the spraying was a huge relief.

Next, basic flying took up our time and again I breezed through it because of my previous training. I spent my free time, while waiting for the other cadets to get caught up with me, in the bowling alley or at the gee-dunk (ice cream) counter in Ships Service (it's called PX nowadays).

Somewhere in these stages we graduated from the bi-plane, N3N, to the Vultee Vibrator, or at least we called it that. I don't think it had retractable landing gear but I could be wrong on that. It was a low-wing, single-engine training plane.

The next step up was to the North American SNJ which definitely did have retractable landing gear. This was a more advanced low-wing trainer. It was also considerably faster than previous training planes. I think the Army Air Corps called it an AT6. Then came instrument flying and my advancing came to a screeching halt--I barely made it through. Oddly enough, years later I became a Navy Instrument Instructor and still later flew in the airlines which requires considerable instrument flying.

# CHAPTER 12
## Decision-making Time

After finally qualifying for instrument flying I had to make a decision whether I wanted to go into advanced multi-engine like P-Boats (sea planes) or single-engine planes like fighters, dive-bombers or torpedo planes. One ride in a P-Boat convinced me no thanks. It was bumpy, slow and too much like driving a bus. I wanted the fun and thrill and speed of a fighter.

When I first flew as a civilian I was captivated by the fun of diving down on clouds and the freedom of twisting and turning in and around them. There was nothing like diving down on to a big puffy white cloud and playing in and around it. I also felt that fighters would be better than torpedo planes because I would have the opportunity to shoot enemy planes down, where torpedo planes don't have that option. After Torpedo Squadron 8 got wiped out at the battle of Midway, I narrowed my choice down to fighters.

My next decision was whether to become a Navy or Marine fighter pilot. My best buddy in training, Walt Stewart, chose the Marines and I almost went with him. Then I thought of the dirt, dust, bugs and heat shore-based guys had to put up with versus the cool living and good meals on board ship, (sounds like a Navy recruiting chief) and chose the Navy.

## CHAPTER 13

### BACK TO TRAINING

I should mention we were thoroughly trained in navigation including celestial and in many other ways such as in aerobatics. I even remember doing an outside loop. Not many pilots do this because it puts pressure on the blood in your brain and maybe could be dangerous. It is the opposite of a regular loop. You nose the plane over and keep pushing the nose further until it starts back up.

I can't recall whether it was in training or later in the fighter squadrons we were taught the "Thach Weave". As I have mentioned, in the early days of the war our fighter, the F4F Grumman Wildcat was inferior to the Japanese Zeros. To counter this Commander Thach devised the "Thach Weave". It was designed to help pilots protect each other's rear end and was used often in escorting bombers. Two fighters separated and then turned into each other which put them head on into the Jap fighter that was tailing the other plane. It was more effective in the early days of the war when our fighter, the F4F (Wildcat) was inferior in every way to Zeros, including the speed. Later we got F6F Hellcats and we could make runs on the enemy planes because among other things the Hellcat was faster.

The different types of gunnery runs were the low-side, where you come up underneath and from the side of the enemy fighter, or high-side, where you make a run usually at a 45 degree angle from above and from the side, and lastly the overhead runs, where you are above the enemy and make a split 'S', rolling over and diving straight down on top of him. In practice we used towed sleeves to shoot at in these runs. I loved the overhead run.

Almost at the end of our overall training and on our last training flight in advanced fighters, we were to fly off from Corpus Christi on a navigation hop over the gulf. This was where I made my first big mistake and I really lived to regret it. Our instructor, because he could not establish contact with the main base radio at Corpus Christi Naval Air station before we took off, instructed me to take charge while he flew back to the base to check in and advise them that we were proceeding on a navigational flight over water. I was supposed to just circle with the other planes flying on my wings until the instructor returned.

Just after the instructor left I spotted a Coast Guard ship and thought what a great chance to practice glide bombing runs (approximately 60 degree dive angle) on the ship. So I led the rest of the planes and we glide-bombed the heck out of that ship. The instructor comes back, sees what is happening and immediately brings all the planes back to base. I can still see the sailors on the cutter running all over the deck, pulling off gun covers because they had no idea who we were or what was happening, why I'll never know. But at that time in the early stages of the war ships were being sunk right off our shores and everybody was gun happy.

Back at the base, we all troop into see the Capitan who was the commanding officer of the unit. Since I was leading the flight and the others just following me, the Captain sent all but me back to our training unit. He proceeded to read me the riot act, threatening to send me to Nome, Alaska at the lowest seaman rate possible for the duration of the war. Apparently the Admiral in charge of the Coast Guard in the area had just read the riot act to him as the officer in charge of the advanced fighter training base. The only thing that saved me was that we had just lost a ton of pilots in the battle of Midway and other battles. Cadets like me were needed badly on the carriers in the Pacific. So I just got three months of marching with a Springfield .06 in good and foul weather.

Ever try carrying a Springfield .06 for hour after hour. It is a rare thing in Corpus, but sometimes we would get a "northerner" and it was bloody cold in my whites carrying that damn rifle. Also, the occasional rain storm didn't help. I wasn't allowed any liberties or foul-weather gear and one time one of the jerk officers caught me chewing gum and added additional marching time. Of course marching in the usual humid summer heat was no fun either, so all-in-all it was a miserable time of my training as I paid the penalty for my escapade.

This dumb move also caused me to lose my seniority, since I didn't graduate till mid January 1943, when I received my Navy Wings of Gold and became an ensign. All my old classmates had graduated and were now senior to me. Thank goodness, they had moved on to the advanced fighter base at Melbourne, Florida, because I would have hated to have to salute them, and I know how much they would have enjoyed it. Ultimately I was moved back some three months in date of rank, making me junior to all the newly commissioned officers in my class. Since the Navy lives and dies by your date of rank it was a big matter for me that affected the rest of my career.

As a sideline here, there was one thing at Corpus that caused me to be an envied cadet. There were umpteen thousand cadets, Navy and Marine officers and enlisted men in and around Corpus Christi and about one thousandth of that number of females. Most of us on liberty just gave up trying to get a date with one of the fairer sex. We were just flat-out out-numbered. But one day I got an idea: I called up a telephone operator and asked if there were any good-looking single telephone operators who might want to go out with an exceedingly handsome, rich and tall young cadet. You would be surprised at how many dates I got. Usually if there were no single operators they would know of someone. None of the cadets could figure out how I did it. When I left I gave the secret to a junior classmate.

How did I get by the lack of being rich, tall, and handsome? Well, I wasn't too ugly and while not tall, I was 5' 10" which in those days was a little taller than most, and I would feed them a line about all the money I had back home. Anyway, by the time I met the gal I was home free. If I met her and she was not what I was looking for, I'd just tell the girl Doug (that's me) couldn't make it. It was kind of like the Machiavellian theory, the end justified the means.

# CHAPTER 14

## THE ENSIGN GOLD BAR AT LAST

When I finally did graduate and got my Ensign's bar and Navy wings of gold I could hardly believe it. I remember walking down a street on the base and having every enlisted man salute me. I thought at first they were making a mistake.

Next, I was shipped to U.S. Naval Air Station Melbourne, Florida. Here I graduated to a real but considerably out-dated fighter plane, the Brewster Buffalo. This plane was the one we sold to the Finnish Air Force to fight the Russians. Incidentally, Commander Winston, commanding officer of the fighter squadron I ended up in combat in the Pacific with, was involved in that program and had ferried a bunch of these to Finland. The plane had a weird characteristic in that it would fly almost sideways like in a perpetual skid, and it looked like a bumble bee. Some of these planes ended up in combat against the Zeros and were badly beaten.

**The Ensign Gold Bars at last.**

Along with the newly commissioned Navy pilots there were English pilots in training at Melbourne. They wore short pants and you could always tell them apart because of all the scars on their legs. They were always wrecking the planes in accidents. They wrecked so many Brewsters that the planes were in short supply. I remember one incident where two British pilots collided and ended up in a swamp near Melbourne standing on their parachutes in the boggy water, fighting over whose fault the accident was. Never mind the alligators, poisonous cotton-mouth moccasins and whatever else, these two limeys were more interested in beating each other up. I guess this attitude prevailed in the Battle of Britain. They had plenty of guts and perseverance.

One of the new pilots I was training with was a New York Italian fellow who was an accomplished ballroom dancer. When he went on leave he would go to Miami to dances where rich and single older ladies were. He only was interested in the older gals and since he was a very good dancer, fairly nice looking and a smooth talker, he was almost always in demand. He looked a little like Don Corleone in "Godfather" and had that New York accent. He used to tell us he was an expert on jewelry so he could spot the really wealthy ones. His said his goal in life was to marry an older rich gal so he could inherit her money when she died. He really fed those old gals a line of BS. I often wondered how he made out in life.

The next step after Melbourne was learning how to land on an aircraft carrier. To do this we were transferred to Norfolk, Virginia, the city that sported all the "No Dogs or Sailors Allowed" signs. Maybe those folks were the grandparents of today's liberal dissidents.

At Norfolk, we flew out of the main airfield to a small outlying field where the runway was marked off to simulate the size of the deck of a small carrier and we were to practice landing on the marked-off space. Since I thought I was such a hot-shot pilot, I didn't pay much attention to the instructions that covered what the landing signal officer (LSO) signals meant because I had already figured it out.

At sea and on the carrier the LSO stands on the port (left) side of the after end of the carrier. For the practice field he stands on the leading, left edge of the marked-off space on the runway, which represents the aft end of the ship, and waves two paddles. If he extends his paddles sideways and level, that's "Roger" and the pilot is flying the plane correctly. If the paddles are high or low, the plane is too high or too low and there are two other signals when the plane is too slow or too fast. Also, of course there is the "cut signal" which is given when all is OK and the plane is in position to land on the carrier, and results in the pilot cutting back the throttles and the plane lands. The last and most important signal is when he waves the paddles overhead in a criss-cross pattern, which signals a wave-off, which means to abort the landing and go around again.

I had some preconceived notion that the idea was to land so the tail wheel touched down as close as possible to the edge of the concrete line marking the ship's stern. WRONG.

On my first and only pass that day I got so slow I spun in and hit the ground from, I guess about 30 feet. I was flying an SNJ, a training plane. It stalls out at a very slow speed which was one reason I survived at all. It also helped that I spun into a huge pile of soft dirt a farmer had plowed up in the field next to the runway. It apparently was just enough to soften the shock of my hitting the ground.

Hard to believe, but I was totally unhurt. I don't even remember my arms bending where I had braced with my hands against the instrument panel. I climbed out of the airplane feeling surprised and really happy that I was in one piece. That's when the LSO took a baseball bat and started chasing me down the runway. He had told us if we wrecked any of his airplanes he was going to beat us up. He had been giving me the "too slow" signal with his paddles and I had not responded to it. I guess I missed that one in class. Anyway I was going to show him by making what I thought was a perfect landing. What I thought was all wrong.

(You have to remember when you are young you are never wrong and you are liable to think you are the hottest pilot in the sky. Later in life when I got married I found out that the part about being right was not always true. As a matter of fact I can't ever remember being right in, now, 58 years of married life.)

Anyway, when I resumed field carrier landing practice you would have had to have a French 75 to shoot me down I was so high. Then an instructor took me up and showed me how to do it and it was a piece of cake. I learned the idea is to land on a carrier so that your tail hook catches about the third wire. The hook catches before the wheels touch the deck and the cable stretches out to slow and eventually stop your forward motion.

# CHAPTER 15

## The Real Thing

Now I was ready for the ultimate test of landing on an actual carrier. The U.S.S. Charger, the smallest carrier in the U.S. fleet was given the task of qualifying new pilots. It was even shorter than the "Jeep" carriers. The top brass figured if we could land on it, we could land on anything. During the North African Invasion it had to turn around and come back due to not being able to handle some bad weather, with heavy seas preventing it from proceeding to North Africa because it was so top-heavy, or at least that's what I heard from someone in ship's company.

In any case about eight of us Navy and Marine pilots headed out from Norfolk Naval Air Station and I wish I could have taped the comments on the radio when we saw the Charger.

From about 5000 feet it looked like a postage stamp and the hollering on the radio from the pilots was really funny. Comments like "I want to go home to mother", and "why did I ever listen to that recruiting chief." As near as I can remember the ship was about 450 feet long with a beam similar in size to "Jeep" carriers. Also as near as I can remember the landing length was only about 250 feet. The landing length of the carrier is shorter than the ship due the length of the fantail (rear of the ship), and the bow had to have room for the barrier. This was several strong wires covered with a lot of canvas that looked like mattress material. This was to stop the plane from going into the drink at the bow of the ship and was positioned a distance aft of the bow for safety and forward of the last wire you could catch to allow barrier wire to stretch. I hope you get the picture.

Most military pilots will agree that there is no other method of landing military aircraft in such a short distance as on an aircraft carrier. Once in awhile you might run into a military pilot other than a Navy or Marine Corps pilot who might not agree with this. You just have to credit it to ignorance or jealousy because he never did it.

Picture that the ship is rolling or pitching and has to be intercepted at the right spot to keep from dragging in on a long straightway aft of the stern. I was only a propeller plane pilot and I understand this may not be a problem for jets today, because their cockpits are near or at the front of the plane and there is no long nose and cowling blocking the pilot's ability to see the LSO like there is on a prop plane. With the propeller planes it is necessary to make a turn at just the right moment to intercept the stern of the ship at the right location so you don't lose sight of the LSO.

Keep in mind 10,000 foot runways are not moving at or about 30 knots, not pitching, nor rolling, nor yawing (a side by side sliding motion.) Our planes were slower than the Navy carrier planes of today, but we landed on carriers anywhere from about 480 feet in length to 888 feet. Today they are like 1000 feet to 1200 feet. The offset to that is that jets land faster than we did, but they have a slanted deck which is almost like another runway and it is kept clear for landings and they can eject if in trouble. We had no such luxuries.

Recently I watched a former Astronaut on TV who was asked which is tougher to land on, the moon or a carrier. He said it's not even close--the carrier is the toughest by far, and night carrier landings were the scariest thing he ever did.

I should add that the single most important thing to do when making an approach to the carrier is to line up right. If you don't you will probably get a wave-off and have to go around again. If you are lined up right it allows you to concentrate on your speed and altitude. If you are too far one side or the other and too close to the ship, the LSO probably won't try to move you left or right but give you a wave-off. If you aren't lined up right it may be too late for the LSO to try and line the plane up right and could create too big a correction, causing the plane to see-saw from side to side, so then it is best to give the pilot a wave-off, directing him to abort and go around and try it again. If you are lined up right the LSO will give you signals to correct your speed, height, or whatever else is wrong. Most seasoned pilots who have made many landings usually end up getting just "roger" signals up to the cut.

I recently had an ex-Air Force officer tell me that while he was observing landings on a carrier he could have done a better job of directing a plane coming aboard than the LSO did, when the plane crashed into the side and rear of the ship. I didn't believe him then and I don't now, because based on his story the proper signal should have been a wave-off, not the banking signal that he claims he advocated, particularly since the pilot was so far off the center line of the ship he ended up hitting its side. I would bet the LSO was giving the pilot a wave-off as he should have been doing. Anyway until you actually land aboard a carrier yourself you are not really in a position to critique landings.

This is particularly true for night landings. I would like to add I never had or heard of an incident where an accident occurred because of poor judgment on the part of an LSO. We pilots had the greatest trust in their skill at directing us with wands and the only accidents I ever heard of were pilot error or due to the pilot or plane being shot up. All LSOs are naval aviators themselves who receive extensive training in bringing pilots aboard ship. We never doubted their judgment.

I haven't talked about the dreaded night carrier landings. In the earliest days of the war and up to the first Philippine Sea battle, where around 100 or so planes returned in the dark without any training in night carrier landings, pilots had not been required to become night-qualified to land aboard ship. After that I understand it became a requirement for at least some to become qualified for night carrier landings, but this wasn't so for me or the guys I served with. I am talking about this being so prior to the end of the war. After the war it became a requirement.

Night carrier landings could be a bit scary mostly because there was little or no light from the ship to see by. Sometimes, but not always, the little light on top of the masthead of the carrier would be on. It always seemed to me that we made these flights when there was little or no moon and I suspicion that the senior officers did it deliberately. The only lights that shone on the deck came from small deck lights on either side of the deck that had like a metal cover over them to shield the light from hitting anywhere but on the deck.

I have somewhere in the vicinity of 100 night landings but all after WWII and all on small jeep carriers (about 480 feet long). The landings seemed to greatly bother some pilots but I guess I was too cocky to be affected. Night landings were tougher than day landings but to me, night or day, each one was like striving for a home run every time you come up to bat. I loved to catch one of the desirable wires and it was something to really aim for, but I won't deny it could be hairy in the dark. The executive officer of one squadron I was in, after his first night landing got out of the plane and refused to do anymore. I don't think that helped him much in his Navy career.

I can remember landing on a carrier so hard I almost wiped out my landing gear. The ship was coming up on a wave and I was coming down from chopping my throttles. Another time I hit a barrier because the hook skipped the wires, jumping all of them. Still another incident, when the squadron skipper (who was new to combat operations but still made skipper because he was a more senior officer than the rest of the pilots) went through or jumped the barrier and hit the rear of my plane, with the prop destroying the rear of the plane all the way up to my armor plate, where he finally stopped. That could have been the end of me. I'm guessing but I think I must have accumulated about 500 day landings, many on the Cabot, a CVL class carrier with the narrowest beam (width). All of the night landings and the rest of the day landings were on various jeep carriers, the smallest carriers in length.

Back to landing on the U.S.S. Charger in Chesapeake Bay, wouldn't you know it, on my first pass the hook pulled out from the plane and I went into the barrier I just described. I was beginning to think I was jinxed. Anyway I got into another plane and got my eight landings qualifying me for the fleet.

It's at this point my memory gets fuzzy. I remember joining a couple of fighter squadrons in the States and the squadron and air groups practicing various attack maneuvers preparing for combat overseas. I do remember, while stationed at Los Alamitos, California preparing to go overseas, dog fighting with the Army Air Corps planes in their P40s, P38s, and the Air Cobra as well as Marine F4U fighters. We had no trouble turning inside the Army Air Corps fighters although the P38, I think, was faster than us.

Often times these dogfights got real low and of course would not be tolerated later after the war. The Marine Corps fighters had an advantage over us in that the F4U was faster than our F6Fs though about the same as far as maneuverability or rate of climb went.

## CHAPTER 16

### THE FUN TIMES

In many ways, this was a romantic time. When we got liberty we spent our time bar-hopping and girl-chasing in San Francisco. A 40's-era best-selling book, "Shore Leave" gave a pretty good idea of our liberty-time activities. This was when most of the males were in the armed service, creating a big shortage of guys available, so we were very busy in the evenings. What's the saying, "you got to make hay while the sun shines". Another one is "so many women--so little time" ( I know ladies, that's a very sexist statement).

I even remember a couple of gals fighting over me and my buddy while we were coming out of a bar, and so help me that's the truth. With millions of guys overseas and all those lonely gals, it was like shooting fish in a rain barrel. The girls really seemed to like guys in uniform. I particularly remember one time when I was going through Washington D.C. at a government cafeteria with a friend in the Navy and there were umpteen hundred government workers (mostly young female secretaries) standing in line. We got more friendly looks than I've probably had ever since.

Sometimes it was boring just training all the time, which consisted of repeatedly practicing tactics and flying to outlying fields from the main base to practice field carrier landings, getting ready for carrier duty. To offset the boredom we would do outlandish things. I'm not sure I should mention this next episode as it might offend some readers. You have to remember we were a little crazy to do the kind of flying we did, and getting bored and eager to go off to combat. So there were times like when a bunch of our squadron's pilots went to a deli and bought large Italian sausages, punctured a hole in them near the end, ran a string through them, then tied them around their waists inside their pants. Then they headed to a dance and as I heard it were the hit of the dance, although there were some stuffy gals who wouldn't have anything to do with them. I'm not going to tell you if I was a part of this or not. Those were the fun days of the war.

From San Francisco we were shipped out on the U.S.S. Lexington to Maui in Hawaii where we trained some more, mostly in making coordinated attacks on enemy ships. One of the most enjoyable and memorable maneuvers that we did while training in the fighter squadrons, before we practiced the coordinated attacks, was the gunnery runs. I used to love doing the gunnery runs.

Before we took off the armory sailors would load our fighters with different colored 50 caliber shells in each plane. This was to identify who hit the target and where on the sleeve. One of the planes would line up on the runway with a tow sleeve about 20 feet in length that was our target. The aircraft mechanic or someone like him would run the sleeve which was attached to a long cable, out as far out as it would go on the runway ahead of the plane. The plane would then take off down the runway and when he had enough speed he would be almost even with the sleeve and would become airborne. Then the target plane with the tow sleeve streaming out behind him would climb to anywhere between 15- and 20,000 feet.

We would make several runs starting either way off to the side, below or above the target. The above runs were called overhead runs and I loved those most of all. We would start the overhead runs by flying ahead and about 2000 feet above the target. Then we would do what is known as the split-S. This was done by rolling the plane over and pointing the nose straight down. We had to lead the target (sleeve) a proper amount so that when our shells got to the target it was there. Also it required us to center the needle on the instrument panel and put the ball to where it and the needle were perfectly centered. If not we would probably be in a skid and our bullets would not go where we aimed them. Of course you had to be careful to lead the target the right amount and start your split-s at the right time so as not to run into the target or the tow cable. When we got back we were real anxious to see how we had done. The pilot with the worst score bought the rest a six pack of beer.

I should mention that all during our training we shot skeet to teach us deflection shooting. This is where you would lead the target, be it skeet or a plane, the proper amount so that the plane or the skeet got there at the same time as the bullets did. You will never hit the target if you aim the bullets straight at a target unless you are right behind it or heading directly into it. This is particularly true if the target is at a big angle to where you are going. This is called deflection shooting.

Back to Maui, where we prepared the squadron for actual combat in the Pacific and where we practiced making coordinated attacks. The attacking planes would fly over a target with the fighters flying high cover while the dive bombers would peel off and dive-bomb the targets. The minute their attack was through, in came the torpedo bombers and lastly, if the fighters had shot down all the enemy planes, they would glide-bomb at 60 degrees, hopefully finishing off as many as possible of the enemy ships. We varied this with the fighters and dive bombers coming into the targets at the same time and this got very hairy with the threat of mid-air collisions. Much of the time, the torpedo bombers would attack ahead of the dive bombers.

Sometimes the fighters and others would skip-bomb ships. This is where we approach the ship at high speed just off the water and drop the bomb just before the enemy ship and hope it skip-bombs into the side of the ship. I had one scary experience doing this that I'll get to later.

All these coordinated attacks have to be timed just right so when one group finishes the next one attacks and it can lead to accidents as we experienced on Maui, losing a couple of good pilots. One was a full-blooded Indian, a Cherokee, I think, good-looking, rugged and very much the handsome- Indian-type guy. I think his last name was Shook. He could have been in the movies.

We felt his loss a lot because he was such a great guy. What a waste.

While on Maui, one of the island residents invited our fighter squadron to a luau. He had a great home right on the beach where you walked right out onto the sand. He said on Pearl Harbor day, December 7, 1941, a Jap submarine surfaced and lobbed some shells at the island. To show how unprepared we where, the only defense that Maui had was one old French 75, World War I-type cannon. However it was on the opposite side of the island and by the time they got it over to the right side the sub was long gone. It's scary how some decisions made by the Jap admirals could have been made in the opposite direction and might have changed the course of the war. The Japanese admirals have been criticized more than once by their own people because they probably could have invaded many of the Hawaiian Islands without much resistance.

# CHAPTER 17

## FINALLY, THE COMBAT ZONE

After a short stay at Maui several of us got transferred from the squadron that was training in Hawaii and sent to the forward areas as replacement pilots to other fighter squadrons in the combat zones. A lot of pilots had been lost in recent battles and replacement pilots were sorely needed. We left Hawaii in a jeep carrier loaded to the hilt with pilots and provisions.

Probably one of the bravest thing or maybe just plain dumb thing I ever did was to volunteer to man a fighter on the catapult one evening when we were thousands of miles from Hawaii and also from our destination in the Central Pacific. The strategy then by our fleet was to bypass a lot of the Japanese stronghold islands and strike at one farther away and closer to Japan, thus effectively neutralizing the by-passed island bases' effectiveness. A major strike against Truk, which has been called the Japanese Pearl Harbor, had done considerable damage. After that, it was completely bypassed by our fleet, rendering it useless to the Japanese forces.

Majuro, an atoll in the Marshall Islands, was our destination, where we were to catch up with the fleet. This was where the fleet had returned from the combat zone to provision with needed supplies. One night, somewhere before we got to our destination, we encountered a "Betty" on our radar scope. This is a two-engine Japanese light bomber similar to the Army Air Corps B-25. If he picked us up on his radar we needed someone to take off from the carrier, intercept and shoot him down before he got to our ship. Our ship was practically defenseless. It had next to no guns, since the deck and hangar decks and every available space were packed to the hilt with planes and supplies.

Once a fighter plane was launched from the ship, there would be no place to land, and since we were traveling without an escorting destroyer or other ship it would be a one-way mission, some 2000 miles from the nearest friendly forces. Since none of us could swim or row in our rubber rafts that far, it was pretty much a suicide mission, Like a dummy I volunteered for it. Fortunately the Jap pilot didn't pick us up and I'm able to write this story now.

You might wonder how the ship protected itself. It had to rely entirely on its speed being faster than the submarines' and traveling on a zigzag pattern, making it difficult for subs to predict a point at which they could intercept it. Most aircraft carriers were able to travel at up to 30 knots and submarines in those days were considerably slower. All escort vessels were needed in the fleets which were in the combat zone, and simply not available to ships being used to supply the fleet.

We finally reached the fleet at Majuro. This was a group of islands and/or atolls where planes and supplies as well as we replacement pilots were off- loaded. Next the Jeep reinforcement carrier launched us off the carrier at anchor, As mentioned, the ship was loaded to the hilt with supplies and planes so we were launched on the catapult at anchor (sitting still) and the air officer had to wait till we got enough wind. I had never heard of launching this way and was a bit apprehensive that it could be done. Don't ask me why they didn't launch us while underway.

Maybe at this point I should mention that planes on an aircraft carrier usually took off by starting at or near the stern and rolling the length of the deck, becoming airborne at or near the bow. If the deck was crowded we would be taxied onto the catapult which was an apparatus that literally slung us into the air in about 75 or so feet and we were then airborne. But now we are sitting on the catapult waiting for enough wind. In order to get airborne at the end of the catapult we needed about 70 to 75 knots. Without it we would stall out and go in the drink. We usually got this by adding the speed of the wind plus the speed of the forward motion of the airplane from the catapult launch and finally the speed of the ship. On normal launches the ship would build up its speed to 30 knots or as close as it could get to that. All of this, under normal conditions, would be enough speed necessary to successfully launch the plane. But now we need enough wind to compensate for the loss of the speed of the ship. So we waited until the wind velocity was enough.

There is one other factor that helped, which was that we were launched about 60 feet above the water. When finally we were launched by the catapult I didn't go in the drink but I sure dipped down towards the sea and below the deck where I was launched. When I went to pick up my flaps only one came up and the plane started to roll, heading for the water. A light went off in my head and I figured if this all happened when I tried to pick up the flaps, I should put them back down.

I flew all the way to the island runway with the flaps down and landed on the metal mat the Seabees had put down. The name of the mat escapes me. You may have read about these mats that the Seabees installed on most of the islands after we captured them. It allowed us to become operational from a field long before a cement field could be constructed, making us ready to attack from that airfield or defend it much sooner.

Majuro was where I joined VF31 (that's fighter squadron 31) aboard the USS Cabot. The Cabot was a converted cruiser around 632 feet long with a very narrow beam due to the cruiser hull. We had maybe 24 fighters and 9 torpedo bombers and no dive bombers.

I discovered to my surprise that a high school friend, Jim Stewart, who had been a couple of years ahead of me in school and was the son of our minister at Beverly Hills Presbyterian Church, was the operations officer in the squadron. He ended up with 9 kills and had a reputation of having a lot of guts, which I saw later in the Philippines when he led a division of 8 planes to attack a heavy cruiser against murderous AA fire. We aren't talking about bombing from 20,000 feet but diving in about a 60 degree dive down almost to the deck, and the AA fire can get real hairy. I was flying over him at the time headed for other targets that I will mention later.

Back to the Cabot, I was put in a room with four crazy guys who didn't seem to sleep at night because they were so busy getting into mischief. We had condoms which were used to put around knives, flashlights and all kinds of survivor equipment for protection from moisture. These were items we carried in the rafts attached to our parachutes. My bunk mates who were always looking for a little excitement would fill the condoms with water so they ended up as water balloons. The bulkheads (walls) were open at the top so they would throw them over the walls through the opening at the top onto someone sleeping on the other side. The ship's air officer was one of these unfortunate souls and did he ever get mad. Of course when he came running around into our room everybody was pretending to be asleep, innocent as newborn babes.

Everybody told me I wouldn't last a week in that room because they didn't ever seem to sleep and I wouldn't either and with 4:00 a.m. musters for pre-dawn fighter sweeps, I needed my rest, so I moved. One other thing they were always doing was to offer $50 or $100 or even more to a bunk mate to go get a gee-dunk (ice cream-made from powdered milk). Then somebody would up those offers to $500 or more, but nobody ever went. Money meant very little because there was nothing to spend it on.

I remember one time one roommate took a trident type spear used for fishing and stuck the point of it between the legs of one of the other roommates while he was sleeping, then woke him up and dared him to move. Funny thing, some of these guys had the most kills in the squadron. Don't ask me how they found the energy. I lasted one week.

There was another clown in the squadron who would call up one of the pilots at all times of the day and night claiming he was the Captain of the ship and he wanted so and so to report immediately to his cabin. So that poor devil would head up to the Captain's quarters. If he happened to disturb the skipper you can imagine how much hell he caught. You can also imagine how apprehensive we were getting this message. The Captain is like a little god on Navy ships and we'd quake in our boots wondering what we'd done wrong. Finally the Captain got onto what was going on and he summoned our culprit to his cabin and read him the riot act.

Before this happened, however, our culprit told the Captain where he could go with his order to report, thinking it was one of his buddies trying to get back at him. This didn't help him much when he finally stood before the skipper. But this was wartime and the skipper probably got a secret laugh out of this, being a good skipper with more important things on his mind. I shudder to think what would have happened to that jokester in peacetime, though.

When I joined the squadron it was while the fleet was anchored at the Majuro atoll. While planes and provisions were being transferred from the Jeep carriers which had brought them from Hawaii or the states, we were allowed to go swimming and visit the small islands in and around the atoll. One day another pilot and I hitched a ride on a shore boat to a deserted little island and went swimming. After that we lay on the island and sunbathed in the nude. The sun in the tropics can be deadly and sun bathing was a big mistake, especially for certain parts of your body. Many of the white-hats and some officers would dive off the side of the carrier which is about 60 feet from the water. It was a kind of a relaxing and fun time, at least for those who weren't sunburned.

I can't remember what campaign we were in when I joined the squadron. I think it had to have been after we conquered the Gilbert and Marshall Islands because Majuro is an atoll in the Marshall group. After that everything is kind of blurred in my memory. I remember being off Espirtu Santo in the New Hebrides. Here, we went ashore and stole a jeep to take a tour of the Island. We got to within binocular range of nurses at the naval hospital there. (Wow!) Driving through the jungle which was incredibly dense on either side of the road we ran over a gigantic boa constrictor that was crossing the road. It almost flipped the jeep. I don't know what we did to the poor snake.

I do remember one island that was the most closely guarded island in the Pacific. They darn near needed traffic cops in airplanes to keep the circling planes from running into each other. It seemed the island had native girls walking around without tops. One of our pilots' bomb rack on his plane malfunctioned, causing a bomb to be accidentally dropped on this island from his plane. Naturally when he got back to the ship the maintenance men painted a partially naked island girl and a palm tree on the side of his plane alongside some 14 Jap Zeros he had shot down. Fortunately he hadn't actually hit anything on the island. They also painted a bunch of gun barrels on the side of his plane because he was always holding the gun trigger down too long and burning up gun barrels. His plane was a sight to see.

# CHAPTER 18

## PALAU–WHERE I ALMOST BOUGHT IT

The next strike I was in happened at Palau in the Central-South Pacific. We had a roommate, a torpedo plane pilot, who had a special talent. He could convince the rest of us that he was getting hot information from someone in CIC (Combat Information Center). This is a large room in a lower part of the ship that is filled with radar and other electronic devices where all the intelligence reports came in. So when we were near Palau he told us two things. First Manny Fujimoto, the number-one Japanese ace and his silver Zero with its 120 American flags printed on its the side, was supposed to be in the area. So watch out if you didn't want to become number 121. Later we found out this was just so much bull. Nobody in CIC ever heard of Manny Fujimoto. This guy was really good at convincing people or we were just gullible. Or maybe we just kind of wanted to believe his crazy stories.

The second item was that the top Japanese Admiral in the Palau area was in one of the buildings we were supposed to bomb. Somebody claimed it was the local whore-house. In any event he described the building so well that I figured I was going to bomb the crap out of it. We later found out that it was true that a top Japanese Admiral was in the locality. We had already cleared out the enemy fighters so now we were due to make a glide-bombing run on the government buildings and anti-aircraft locations.

Frequently on these local islands the Japanese would put long narrow cement walkways out into the water and at the end there would be a circular structure housing a bunch of anti-aircraft machine gun nests. (Years later when one of my friends visited one of the islands in the Palau group he walked out on what was left of one of these former wartime machine gun nests. He proceeded to write on a wall "This is the place where Commander Doug McLaughlin won the war". I just hope none of my wartime buddies ever see this.

I'm not sure if the reader will understand this as I attempt to explain how we make glide-bombing runs, but I will try anyway. Before the run we usually would fly in formations of four planes with number two flying on number one's wing and number four flying on number three's wing. This is called a division as near as I can remember. Eight planes were just two divisions and 16 were four divisions. Normally when we glide-bombed we dove separately but we could also dive in formation. If we dove in formation you had to keep your eyes on the plane next to you as you dove. This is tough to do and keep the needle and ball on the instrument panel in the middle as well. If they aren't in the middle the bomb will not go to whatever you are aiming at and you will be diving in a skid.

We took off from the ship with about 12--18 fighters, I can't remember which, on this bombing run. We usually did this after the enemy fighters had all been destroyed. In this case our leader had decided to bomb in formation because he could bring to bear six fifty-caliber guns per each plane diving on the machine gun nests and the rest of the targets, totaling 72 to 108 guns in all, as opposed to only six guns per run using one plane at a time. This causes the AA nests to sometimes remain silent while being strafed by all those planes with so many guns, so as not to expose themselves as targets. This all changes when our planes pull up. So, this day they decided to glide bomb in formation, but I decided to make a solo dive so I could keep my needle and ball really centered, giving me a much better chance of hitting the target. DUMB IDEA.

I waited until the rest of the squadron had completed its run, then began my dive and all of a sudden every gun on the island opened up. The exploding shells were so thick it looked like the Black Forest of Germany. I dropped my bomb and hoped to hell I had hit that building with the Jap Admiral in it and pulled out, but somewhere during the dive the plane was hit by AA fire (Anti-Aircraft fire). It knocked out all of my hydraulic lines when it exploded right outside the cockpit. I have no idea why it didn't hit me because there are about six hydraulic lines running horizontally along the inside of my cockpit that were busted, with hydraulic fluid all over the cockpit, in my eyes and all my clothes. Hydraulic fluid is very viscous and next-to impossible to clean out of anything.

I couldn't see and I had to land aboard the carrier. I called to one of the pilots to direct me up or down or left or right while I tried to get the fluid out of my eyes and fly the plane back to the ship. The other plane led me back to the carrier. It was like flying blind or flying on instruments only. The ship instructed me to circle to burn up fuel because, as they put it, they didn't want me to hit the deck and turn into a ball of fire. I thanked them for their confidence and kind words and told them I also would prefer not to end up in a ball of flame. So I was given a choice of ditching into the water and taking my chances with the sharks and maybe being captured by the enemy or maybe if a friendly sub was in the area to be picked up by him. Of course there is no guarantee that this would happen. I had a handkerchief that had the map of the area showing water currents, and other such information on the area where we were in case we went into the drink, and I used this to try and get the hydraulic fluid out of my eyes. Keep in mind we are in unfriendly waters with the Japanese in control of the islands. The big ships could not stop to pick me up because of the risk of becoming a sitting duck for subs. I had to hope one of our subs would pick me up if I went in the drink since it was about 2,000 miles to friendly faces. This didn't appeal to me, so I opted to land on the carrier.

Even with the hanky it took about two hours before I could halfway see. Finally, when I was down to almost only vapor for fuel I made my approach. I should mention an approach to landing on a carrier is done by initially flying above and on the starboard side of the carrier at 400 to 500 foot altitude, proceeding past the carrier and going forward of it a ways and then beginning to lose altitude and turning left, crossing the carrier's course ahead of it. At a prescribed distance ahead and to the port side you turn again to the left and slow down and lose altitude to about 200 feet at somewhere around 90 knots of speed. At this point you want to begin dropping your flaps and landing gear as well as the tail hook. You are now going in the opposite direction to the carrier's course and when you reach about even with the carrier's stern begin a turn to the left and final approach, slowing still further and you should be about 80 to 90 feet in altitude, I guess, since you do this mostly by feel. Next, straighten up, following the landing signal officer's directions with his paddles, or lights at night, and when he gives you a cut (one paddle cutting across his neck) you pull back on the throttle and wait for the tail hook to catch a wire that is stretched across the deck. It will catch before the wheels touch the deck, since the hook hangs down lower than the wheels on the plane. To this day I'm not certain if I ever saw the LSO give me the cut. I had no choice anyway but to take the cut because there just wasn't any more fuel left for me to even go around again.

It was extra tough because not only did the hydraulic system not work, which actuated the flaps and landing gear, but the air backup system did not work either, causing the flaps to not come down. This meant that I was going to have to land a lot faster than normal and have to hold one wing up, because only one wheel came down. In those days most of the planes actuated their landing gear, wing flaps, and maybe even the cowl flaps by hydraulic pressure.

Normally I would have had an air pressure system to back up the hydraulic system but in this case the tank for it had been shot up so that almost nothing worked except the engine. The reason I had to land faster was because the flaps wouldn't come down and they give the plane added lift because they extend the wing surface. More importantly, it lowers the stalling speed of the plane to have flaps down. Without flaps the plane has less lift, consequently it has a higher stalling speed. Having only one wheel extend wasn't a problem because once the other plane who had accompanied me told me which wheel didn't extend I held the wing up and the plane caught a wire and the wing came down skidding along the deck, but held to a fairly straight path by the hook and other wheel.

Have you ever felt real powerful and really in control? In order for me to land on the carrier it had to turn into the wind in order to give me maximum wind over the deck. Because that carrier could not go out of the formation in the task force and become meat for the Jap subs, all the ships had to turn into the wind in order to keep protecting each other just to land little ol' me. Thousands on thousands are involved in manning these ships because of me. Hey,

I'm King for a day. Anyway I landed somehow and went to the ready room. After landing, pilots are briefed by the LSO on how he rated their landings. When I came into the ready room the LSO shouted "McLaughlin, I hope you get your ass shot up every time because that was the best damn landing you ever made."

## CHAPTER 19

### THE ULITHI STORM

The next engagement I was involved in was the battles around Saipan, Tinian, and Guam, known today as the Marianas Turkey Shoot. Before I get into that though, I've got to interrupt myself to tell about the infamous typhoon off Ulithi. We may have lost more planes from that typhoon than in the entire war. We can probably blame Admiral "Bull" Halsey for this debacle. In later years in reading various books, particularly "Wings of Gold" by Gerald Astor, an excellent book detailing the war in the Pacific, General McArthur requested that Halsey provide air cover for some of his invasion forces near New Guinea. Halsey's aerologists (Navy's name in those days for meteorologist) warned him that to do so would take us right through a fearsome storm system. He disregarded the advice and went anyway. Maybe that's why his nickname was "Bull" Halsey. His bull-headed decision ended up causing devastating damage to the third fleet.

Aboard our carrier, the Cabot, some of us pilots were sitting in the wardroom, which is a very large room where we ate and played cards. All of a sudden all the tables and personnel went flying to one end of the wardroom. I wanted to know what was going on, so I went outside along the catwalk that runs on either side of the landing deck. The seas were enough to scare the wits out of you. The Cabot is about 632 feet long and we looked like a surf board going down a wave. I got more scared looking at those seas than in most of my air engagements.

While I'm thinking about it don't ever let anybody tell you that they never got scared while in combat. Most times you are so busy handling the plane you don't have time to get scared. It's when you have no control over what's happening that the fear can get to you. Once, I was running on the deck of the carrier trying to get to the catwalk to escape whatever it was that was attacking us, which today I don't remember, when all of a sudden I couldn't move my legs. I had to physically take my leg with my hand and move it. I don't remember anything else about what was happening because my mind blanked it out. Years later when a German shepherd attacked my two little dogs, rage did a similar thing to me—I totally blanked out and came to lying on top of the shepherd with my hands around its throat. But back to being scared, it's how you handle it that counts. As long as you can ignore it and do whatever you have to do, you're fine.

Anyway, I was digressing. My wife says I do that too much. So, back to the typhoon. Ship's personnel were running around the deck trying to tie the planes down. Some planes had broken loose from their tie-downs and gone over the side of the ship. The deck was wood in those days and there was lots of oil on the deck making it very slippery. During flight operations with the propellers turning this could make it really dangerous trying to walk between those turning props. Naturally there were no flight operations during the storm, but those sliding planes had to be a menace to the crew.

Later I heard three cans (three hundred and fifty foot destroyers) rolled completely over in the storm, and all hands were lost. I don't know exactly, but I believe one can's crew would be around 300. I think later this was called the "Ulithi Storm" when it was written up in history books.

I read in "Wings of Gold" that Halsey was supposed to be brought up on charges for disregarding the storm warnings and causing such loss of men and materiel. Due to his fame and being labeled a hero in the eyes of the public it never happened. He did something similar again later in the war when he took off with the fleet to chase what he thought was the Japanese fleet to the north. The actual Jap fleet had snookered him and gone south, where it caught our weakly protected invasion fleet--jeep carriers, destroyers and other lighter ships. The Japanese did a number on those baby flattops and other ships with their big battleships and heavy cruisers.

The fleet that took all that punishment was part of the invasion fleet that normally fell in behind task force 58/38 in attacking Japanese-controlled islands and provided the invasion with men and equipment, after the third or fifth fleet, with its larger carriers and battleships had pretty much cleared the way for them. Halsey got in trouble for this but once again his fame saved him. I think it was during this same engagement that President Jack Kennedy became something of hero with his PT boat attacking far larger ships than his.

# CHAPTER 20
## THE MARIANAS TURKEY SHOOT

Getting back to the "Marianas Turkey Shoot", which was named for the big air battle in and around Saipan, Tinian, and Guam: What happened was that the Japanese decided that in our island-hopping we were getting too close to Japan and they were afraid that we might get close enough with long-range land bombers to become a threat to their homeland. So they decided to gather their navy and army aircraft nearby in one gigantic force to stop and defeat us at the islands mentioned above.

Three to four hundred or more planes from Japanese carriers to the west of us took off to attack us. There were also land-based Japanese planes from nearby airfields that joined the Japanese carrier-based navy fighter aircraft to

*Rambling Memories*

attack us in one big battle. The Jap carrier planes were to land at airfields on one of the islands. Japanese planes from the north joined them also and we had a huge air battle on our hands. All our fighters were scrambled and given certain sectors around the fleet and directed to about angels 25 (25,000 feet).

Wouldn't you know it, my wingman's oxygen failed and we had to remain at or below 10,000 feet, where nothing happened. So we sat and circled, watching Jap planes falling all around us like flies. I was told after the battle some 350 to 400 Japanese planes were shot down that day. In some other engagements during the war both in the Pacific and European theatres there may have been more planes involved although I am not certain of this, but in this case just about all the Japanese planes were fighter planes.

Losing this many fighters was a huge loss to the Japanese, particularly losing the pilots. The Japanese really felt this later in the war. Some of our fighters went over to the Japanese-held airfields and shot down their planes landing or taking off. It was a huge victory for our side and very badly weakened the Japanese naval and army air forces. One of our Navy pilots shot down six in one flight. That equaled or bettered Butch O'Hare, the posthumously awarded Medal of Honor winner, a Navy fighter pilot who fought in the earlier part of the war during the battle of Midway.

There were all sorts of heroes that day. Our Navy fighter planes that went over to the airfields that the Japs held had some of the highest number of kills because the Jap planes were so vulnerable when landing or taking off. Other individuals encountered various Jap planes all over the place and ended up shooting them down. I felt really unlucky because I hadn't been able to participate and gotten myself some kills. When you are young you never think that maybe you might buy it instead of the enemy. After awhile you begin to think that shooting planes down is made up of two factors, being aggressive and being lucky, because you are in the right place at the right time and you capitalize on it.

# CHAPTER 21

## FLIGHT INTO DARKNESS

Following this battle, our submarines picked up the main body of the Japanese fleet about 300-400 miles to the west of our fleet. These were the carriers who had launched the fighters mentioned previously. Having lost most of their planes, particularly the Zeros, they were running away to the West at flank speed. It was about 3:00 or 4:00 in the afternoon and for us to mount an air attack would mean we would be returning after dark and really low on fuel, since we would have to go not only the distance of 300-plus miles to get to the enemy but also cover the distance the Jap fleet made during the elapsed time until we could intercept them. Then of course we would use up fuel fighting the enemy fighters and we also had to have enough fuel for the return flight.

Our planes were not large bombers with high fuel capacity but instead small single-engine fighters, dive bombers, and torpedo planes. While they were all fitted with auxiliary tanks, usually under the belly or wings, it was still a limited amount of fuel because the belly tanks didn't carry much. Also, often you had to drop the extra tank if it was necessary to have extra speed like in a dog fight, because the tank slowed the plane down due to its air resistance. Thus you might not have been able to depend on the use of all the fuel in the extra wing or belly tank.

Our Admiral decided to go for it. After reading "Wings of Gold", by Gerald Astor, which provides excellent coverage of all these happenings because Astor interviewed hundreds of Navy and Marine pilots and high-ranking officers, I read this flight wasn't really necessary. If Admiral Spruance, Commander of the Fleet, had only listened to Rear Admiral Marc A. Mitscher, commander of Task Force 58, who, along with one of our fighter plane squadron skippers, begged him to direct the fleet the day before to head towards the west and the Jap fleet, it would have narrowed the distance so that the flight into darkness, as some have called it, may not have been necessary.

Anyway, Admiral Mitscher issued orders and the planes took off a day later, late in the day, with his blessings.

There were roughly 700 planes in the task force, and squadrons were rotated on missions. There must have been something in excess of 100 planes that took off and attacked the enemy ships far to the West of us. My own squadron wasn't one of those sent out. Some got engaged in shooting down what Jap fighters that were left behind to protect their carriers and the rest of the guys bombed and torpedoed the enemy, scoring many hits. Upon return it was way after nightfall, with no moon, making it extremely dark. All or most of our pilots had never made a night landing so it was real tough, with some pilots almost landing on destroyers or cruisers.

I remember a flight of about six planes in formation circling our ship too low because the last plane, which was flying wing on another plane, hit the drink. When you are flying formation your whole concentration is on flying on the plane off your wing. The plane flying last in the formation hit the water and cart-wheeled and to this day I can still see him spinning into the sea while I thought what a shame to die that way. At least, he probably never knew what hit him. The fault for that loss was the leader's, who flew too low. But then he too had lots of problems flying around in the dark trying to find and land aboard a carrier, with no prior night landing experience.

The worst problem that reared its ugly head was that 40 to 50 planes ran out of fuel before they got back to the carriers and had to ditch into the sea. Most of the pilots were able to get out of their planes and into the life rafts that they carried. Many were later picked up by subs or destroyers, but not all were saved. It showed the concern our superiors had for their men when the entire fleet turned in the direction of the downed pilots to make it easier to save as many as possible. I think the worst thing I could imagine was to go into the drink and become shark bait.

A gutsy thing Admiral Mitscher did was to turn on all the lights in the fleet to help our pilots see where to land. Years later I made many night landings and the only lights allowed, due to submarine threat, were dust-pan lights that point directly at the deck, with a cover to prevent any rays of light from shining anywhere else. There actually were enemy planes around the fleet, so it was gutsy to turn on all those lights from that standpoint, but the biggest threat came from exposure to Jap submarines.

One of our torpedo bomber pilots was in the sick bay on one of the big carriers because he had crashed on landing. Several of his buddies went over to the ship to see him when we were at anchor later and they reported there was a Japanese Navy plane tied down on the deck with a Marine guarding it. The story was that Jap pilot got disoriented and may have thought the American ship was one of his, or maybe was just low on fuel. In any case, he landed aboard our U.S. carrier. According to guys on the ship, he and an American plane took cuts from the Landing Signal Officer at almost the same time, with one plane catching a later wire on the deck. I never tried to verify this but our visiting pilots swore this was true.

## CHAPTER 22

### SURVIVAL STORIES

---

One of the things the Navy did was to provide us with all kinds of survival gear in our life rafts. The raft was secured to our parachute and in the event you went into the water you just pulled the lanyard, inflating the raft. There was a little flashlight, a knife for spearing fish if you were able to, fish hooks, suntan lotion and more that I just don't remember any more. One of our pilots, we called him Red, went in the drink and after being rescued told us of his experiences. He ended up watching air battles and, I think, also sea battles while in the raft in the water. He ate raw fish and one too- curious bird that landed on his raft. I think one of our subs picked him up. One of the items that protected his survival gear was that everything was kept in condoms--kind of a strange use of the product, but very effective, I guess. He said you would be surprised at how hungry you could get after a few days floating around on the raft, which was the reason he ate the bird. I think his raft had ample water provisions but not food.

That's another thing that we had over the Japanese pilots. In addition to our having self-sealing fuel tanks and armor plate behind our cockpit to protect us, there was this attitude to make every effort to recover downed pilots. This was usually accomplished by submarines. It made us pilots feel much better about our chances of survival. I don't believe the Japanese were as caring of their pilots.

Our first President Bush was picked up by a submarine when he was shot down near the island of Chichi Jima, during attacks later in the war on Iwo Jima. He had been flying a TBM, which was a torpedo plane.

## CHAPTER 23
## THE FIGHT GOES ON

After attacking and wiping out most of the enemy fighters at Saipan, Tinian and Guam, we now had control of the skies, so once the invasion fleet was replenished with the necessary supplies, it moved in and began assaults on the three islands. This was another huge fleet made up of jeep carriers (the small ones) and troop transports, supply ships, destroyers and other warships.

Of course all during this time we were making bombing runs on various Jap targets, plus strafing runs on shore fortifications, although the latter was normally handled by the jeep carriers' planes. I wasn't keeping very good log books during these times, and 60-some years later I can't remember specific strikes I was involved in, but I do remember coming back to the ship a few times with holes in my plane, so I must have been doing something right. Years later when I thought about it I didn't understand why I didn't get shook up from all those times the enemy was shooting at me and frequently hitting my plane. I guess it was because I was young and invincible, at least in my mind. Also in that war there was a lot of anger at the Japs for what they had done which seem to erase your own feelings because I truly don't remember being scared very often.

Back to the invasion of the three islands, Saipan, Tinian, and Guam by the Marines and Army troops. This resulted in high casualty figures that were downright brutal. On one of the islands, I think it was Tinian, thousands of Japanese and I think some natives jumped to their death off cliffs. They were determined not to be captured. They had been told horror stories about what the Americans would do to them if they were caught. The Japanese dedication to stopping our forces was intense, with the enemy really dug in. I guess the invasions of the three islands rivaled the Normandy invasion in the fierce fighting and number of losses.

Before we left the islands we had a chance to go ashore, where we saw Marines guarding prisoners who were dressed in what looked like diapers and sandals and that was all. The thing that struck me was how small the Japanese prisoners were. All of them looked like they were less than five feet tall. We were told the reason they were stripped down to the diaper-like garments was that the Japanese were very adept at concealing weapons. I understand that nowadays because of their healthier diet, they are one of the fastest-growing people in height in the world.

We were told when we went ashore to be sure and carry the .38 revolver that we always wore in a shoulder holster while flying, because not all of the island was secured and enemy snipers were everywhere.

*My flight division on the carrier deck (USS Cabot) in the South Pacific in 1944 with a couple of replacements. I'm the pilot on the far left.*

# CHAPTER 24

## How It's Done

To give you an idea of a strike and what we went through when we attacked enemy locations I will use the following attack on Iwo Jima to explain what we did. It was pretty similar to most of our other engagements where we were attacking a Japanese-held target for the first or second time.

Now we leave for the surprise attack, we hope, on Iwo Jima. I will never forget that little bunch of islands. To me they were the most heavily fortified islands in the Pacific and I think it was where we suffered some of our heaviest casualties. Iwo Jima is only around 500 miles south of Japan so the Japanese were very determined to stop our advance toward their homeland and they put up very stiff resistance.

We would take off from the ship with about 18 fighter planes, if my memory serves me right, and return with about ten or twelve. It was really brought home to us when we sat down to dinner at night in the ward room and saw the empty chairs. I know it isn't as rough as the marines and soldiers had to put up with, fighting hand-to-hand in the jungle and having to see the blood and gore, but it was hard seeing your fellow pilot's chair empty at the dinner table and knowing he was gone forever.

Our initial strike was made up of only fighters. Later the dive bombers and torpedo bombers struck the islands. This was supposed to be after we had cleaned out all the enemy fighters. We were told by our CIC (Combat Information Center) officers that the surviving Japanese fighter pilots who had been in the earlier battles such as Battle of Midway and Coral Sea had come down from Japan, because we were only 500 or so miles south of there. They were supposed to be the cream of the crop and it sure turned out that way. They were very determined to stop the advance of our forces and fought fiercely.

The Western and Central Pacific islands that were occupied by the Japanese had been guarded by them for years, allowing no foreign visitors. Thus virtually no information about them had ever been released. The Japanese were paranoid about maintaining this secrecy. Some say the reason Amelia Earhart was never found was because the Japanese forbade any searches on these islands. Earhart was a famous woman pilot of her day who was trying to fly around the world in the 1930s and was lost over the Pacific.

All we had in the way of charts for recognition were copies of National Geographic Magazine maps that outlined the shapes of the islands. We were each given these to help us locate targets. I still have a mental picture of these simple maps and the group of islands they showed. Iwo Jima was the largest. Chichi Jima, where Bush was shot down, was smaller and to the north.

# CHAPTER 25

## A Day In The Life Of A Pilot

---

Around four or five in the morning of July 4, 1944 I was awakened to get up for early breakfast and preparation for pre-dawn take-off. The corridors and rooms where we went on the ship for breakfast were lit in a red glow for our night-blindness control. I can still see those dimly lit rooms and corridors lit only in a dim red color to help us with night vision. I always hated having breakfast before dawn. It is hard enough to get up at a 4:00 a.m. to be served some hash that most of us had trouble even thinking about eating. Still, I know if some ground jockey like a Marine or soldier reads this he'll probably say "poor baby" or something similar, and I'd have to agree that they had it a lot tougher than we did.

After breakfast we went to the pilots' ready room for pre-flight briefing. This is where the flight gear like Mae West, (life jackets), oxygen masks, chart boards and all the rest of the stuff we wore when flying the airplanes was stowed. Chart boards were like large square-shaped Plexiglas-type boards with a 360-degree, circular-shaped wheel that you could spin in any direction mounted on top of the board. This was called the plotting board. It was stowed directly under the bottom of the instrument panel and was pulled out into our laps to use. We had to operate this while flying the fighter, which wasn't all that easy.

Before take-off, we would insert the wind figures based on expected winds at the altitude we would be flying at on the board, and then correct them, if necessary, when airborne. As I recall there was a formula for so many feet of altitude affecting the speed of the wind. Then of course the direction of the wind could change and we didn't have a weather station to go to get our winds aloft. I seem to remember that the aerologist we had on board ship sent weather balloons aloft to help us with the direction and speed of the winds at our prescribed altitude.

In order to plot our course we had to correct the headings for deviation, which is the error inherent in the plane's compass. We also had a magnetic variation to correct. This is a correction due to the difference in the location of the magnetic North Pole and the location of the true North Pole. Because the compass is drawn to the magnetic pole, which is where large deposits of magnetic metals create a magnetic pull, it doesn't actually indicate true north. The difference is a known figure that varies according to location and is shown on charts all over the world. For example, if memory serves me right, the variation figure for Southern California in one area is 15 degrees. Knowing this, one simply subtracts (I think subtracts is right--it has been so long) the 15 degrees from the true course to arrive at the magnetic course. By applying the deviation figure mentioned earlier to the magnetic course you now have the compass course. Put this course on the plotting board and apply a wind factor and away you go. It seemed to me that the circles on the wheel of the plotting board we rotated represented the speed of the plane.

Next we would be briefed by our intelligence officers on targets, what enemy resistance to expect over the target and general strength of the enemy. Our July Fourth pre-dawn strike would be one of the first that any American planes had ever flown over Iwo and Chichi Jima islands. Up until recently I thought this flight was the first-ever flight over Iwo. After having read "Wings of Gold" I discovered that

VF--1, my old squadron that I'd been transferred out of from Hawaii as a replacement pilot, had struck Iwo a month earlier.

We only had guesses on what was there and what to expect. I mentioned before that rumor had it we were going to meet the cream-of-the crop Japanese pilots who had survived earlier battles. This came straight from CIC itself, not our story-telling shipmate with his "Manny Fujimoto" yarns. It turned out to be right.

(Before I forget, the reason we called our life jackets "Mae West" was when inflated they had a resemblance to the figure of a more than well endowed movie star famous in the 30's and 40's and still not forgotten.) I have described our life rafts and how they were equipped. We sat on them and they were hooked to our parachutes. When you think about it we were pretty heavily weighted down.

After all our preparations the waiting is over and we hear "Pilots, man your planes". We go trooping out onto the flight deck and climb in the cockpit. Most of the time we didn't have to dodge whirling propellers but it could happen if you were one of the last to head for your plane before the next bullhorn call, "Pilots start your engines".

For this pre-dawn take-off it is still pitch-black outside. While we are manning our planes, the carrier and other ships are turning into the wind for take-off. I don't remember for sure but I don't think this was a deck launch but rather a catapult launch. So, when it is our turn we taxi up to the catapult by following the directions of a deck crewman with wands (because it is still at night) and wait to be tied down to the catapult. Think of a catapult like it is a sling shot. The deck crewman off my starboard wing who gives the signal to the catapult officer to launch me will wait until there has been sufficient interval between me and the previous plane launched. Then he will whirl his wand in a circular style. I push my throttle to the limit, give him a hand salute and then he or someone else pushes the catapult button and away we go.

The waiting interval between launches was because it could be a problem if you were too close to the plane ahead and ran into his prop wash when airborne, which might throw the plane into an attitude that could be dangerous at such a low altitude just after launching.

The catapult is a gigantic hydraulic cylinder under the deck using hydraulic liquid under extreme pressure that actuates a big piston. The plane is literally flung into the air after traveling along about 75 feet of catapult. I believe today they use steam pressure.

To digress for a moment, years later when I served as a senior aviator on cruisers and battleships, my SC, a single engine, low-wing seaplane, was thrown into the air in a much shorter distance by a catapult, using a six-inch shell. It's more of a jolt.

Back to July 4, once I am launched and after picking up my wheels and flaps I begin my rendezvous with the rest of the planes. This is done by the lead plane flying straight ahead a suitable distance farther than any of the other planes will fly. He then makes a 180 degree turn to the left, to a position where he is flying in the opposite direction, back towards the carrier. He won't begin his turn until he has gone a distance estimated to be far enough to allow all the planes flying behind him to make their turns. The more planes, the greater distance he goes before beginning his turn.

Then he flies parallel to the carrier's course but still up ahead of it, and headed back toward the carrier. Upon being launched, each plane flies ahead and begins a 180 degree turn back towards the carrier at a point where he can intercept the plane ahead. Eventually the whole flight joins up. This occurs about the time they reach the carrier, passing the ship going in an opposite direction.

Somehow another plane and I missed the rendezvous in the dark. Since we weren't allowed any lights we flew off the exhaust flame of the plane ahead. Of course, like all night and pre-dawn flights it was moonless, and darker than the inside of a goat. One of the reasons we missed the rendezvous point was that the plane flying on my wing was a plane I was supposed to be flying on rather than the other way around. I kept trying to get him to take the lead and he kept saying forget it and by the time we got that squared away the main body of planes was long gone.

Since we had missed the main body of the flight I took the lead and flew directly to Iwo Jima, and ended up reaching the island ahead of the main body of planes.

Because I was leading I always figured I was the first American to fly over Iwo Jima, not that it mattered to anybody but me. But years later, in "Wings of Gold", I read that another Navy fighter squadron, VF1, had attacked Iwo one month earlier, so I lost my big distinction.

Back to the action: We were at about 25,000 feet over Iwo Jima, which is a very small island in a cluster of small islands. The Japs were shooting a ton of AA (anti-aircraft-fire) at us. It seemed weird that they would waste so much ammunition on two little fighter planes just circling their island, not hurting anybody. The AA just seemed to be following us around as we circled and waited, not hitting us. Finally the main body of fighters showed up and we joined them. I think the total number of our planes was about 18 F6F-Hellcat fighters. Next all of a sudden 4 or 5 Jap fighters showed up to the left and to the right and slightly below us. Our leader shoved the throttle to the wall and went after them and we all followed.

The enemy was doing slow rolls and loops trying to entice us. That should have been a clue that they were planning something devious. Then they split, and one bunch went in a steep dive to the right and ended up on the northeast side of another small island to our right. This was the direction I went. As we approached the island, the enemy planes disappeared behind it. There were about 40 Jap fighters that had been hidden behind the mountain on the island who were waiting to pounce on us.

The other enemy planes went back and to the left of us in a steep dive pulling some of our planes after them. They flew low over the airfield with some of our planes chasing them. The enemy AA fire was silent while they went over the field

*Rambling Memories*

but opened up really heavy when our planes went over, shooting down several of ours, mostly because our planes were so low. I guess it was true that the Japanese pilots we met were some of their mighty good pilots because they sure snookered us. It also didn't help that Iwo Jima was so heavily fortified. It had more anti-aircraft guns than any island I ever attacked. Not a very friendly place.

Back to me, I spotted a Jap plane shooting heavily at the tail of one of our planes below me. I opened up on him and he turned, climbing and heading directly at me. I kept pouring fire into him as I dove on him and he burst into flames. Every sixth shell is a tracer so it is easy to see where your bullets are going. Looking back I saw a column of smoke where I guess he hit the water.

One of the oddities of this episode was that I hesitated in firing on him because he was brown in color, apparently a Japanese Army Air Corps plane and the wrong color for a Navy Zero. He looked a lot like a P40 but there was no way that could be, since the U.S. Army Air Corps was nowhere near this part of the world. So I came to my senses and fired on him. While I was firing on him he was firing at me as we were heading at each other. It was almost like we were playing chicken. Anyway my bullets hit him often enough while his were mostly tracers going over and under my wings that he lost in the battle of "chicken".

It turned out later that this plane I shot down was attacking our squadron's leading ace, who by war's end was credited with 22 kills. He later confirmed my kill. This may have been my biggest contribution to the war effort.

While I was busy with this guy, somebody had got on my tail and tracers were going over my wing. Knowing that if I turned he would cut inside me because he was more maneuverable than me and staying on my tail pouring his 20 millimeter canon shells into me, I just jammed the throttle to the firewall, trimmed the cowl flaps, turned on the water injection and prayed I could outrun him. Water injection gives you an extra 100 to 200 horsepower. Also, at some point, I had dropped my belly tank to give me more speed.

# CHAPTER 26

## CLOSE ENCOUNTER OF THE WRONG KIND

Eventually I did outrun him, but now I was way north of Iwo and no friendlies in sight. It was a very lonely feeling being 500 or so miles south of Japan and not exactly sure where I was. Dog-fighting over a vast expanse of water can do that to you.

Thinking that Iwo was southwest of my present position, I turned and headed in that direction. I didn't want to get caught too low or too slow, so I began a moderate climb and speed for altitude. In trying to escape the guy on my tail I had dived all the way to the deck and was just above the waves when I finally lost him. So now I am climbing through around 20,000 feet, when off to my right I spot four planes with belly tanks.

When your closing rate between friend and foe can be 700 to 800 miles per hour (350-400 per plane) it is often difficult to tell who is who. Later the Americans developed an electronic device for quick identification of friend from foe. I'm not sure but we might have had that then, but I think it may have only been good between a plane and a ship. Sometimes in the heat of battle we would get shot at by our own ships. Anyway, It was called IFF (Identification Friend or Foe).

One of the strongest recognition features to distinguish U.S. and Japanese planes was that normally our planes had a belly tank because they were usually coming from a carrier 200-300 miles from the island we were attacking. The Japanese planes didn't need the extra gas because they were usually intercepting us near or over their own land bases. In this case the planes must have been coming down from Japan to reinforce Iwo Jima and due to the long distance, needed the extra gas to make the flight.

My first reaction was to join up and rendezvous with them, sending God a little "thank you" prayer. Seeing me at a distance with no extra belly tank, they must have thought I was Japanese so they turned towards me to help me join up. Meanwhile, I continued my turning to join up when all of a sudden I saw the big red meatball on the side of a plane about the same time they recognized I was not Japanese.

Since I had pointed the plane directly at a position to place me on the wing of the last plane so I could join on him and being very close, I just pressed the gun trigger and he flew into a hail of 50-caliber bullets, exploding almost instantly. It was a classic deflection shot. Unfortunately, since no one saw this and my gun camera didn't work I didn't get credit for this kill.

Next I looked up above and the three remaining planes were doing a loop over onto my tail. Near as I can remember, I pulled up and blasted the last of those three planes before the other two looped onto my tail. I couldn't believe how quick they were. From then on in I was a firm believer in the maneuverability of the Jap Zero.

Later on when I got back to the ship, one of the other fighter pilots said, after I told him I had broken off dog-fighting with the last two Zeros, that he would have continued dog-fighting them. I noticed after the next engagement that he was in that he was missing. I remembered a saying I'd heard somewhere: "It's best to fight and get away, so you can live to fight another day."

Back to my dilemma: One of the few times I paid attention in class I had learned that we had an advantage over the Zeros in that we had hydraulic or maybe it was electrically operated trim tabs and they didn't. Trim tabs are small metal fins that stick out from various surfaces like a rudder or vertical stabilizers and help pull those airfoils in the direction the pilot chooses. About the time I had gone into a dive with those two zeros on my tail and tracers going over my wings again, I needed an escape plan.

When planes go into dives they pick up so much speed that the controls tend to freeze up on them. Since it is the natural tendency for the plane with props to turn to the left in high speeds, because that is the direction of the torque of the plane, it is really hard to turn the plane to the right. To explain it another way, the propeller rotates to the right and it becomes a very strong force, pulling the plane to the left at high speeds. Somehow I remembered about the trim tabs, so I went into a high-speed dive and turned to the right, allowing me to eventually get away from the Zeros since they didn't have the trim tabs and couldn't turn to the right in a high-speed dive.

# CHAPTER 27
## GETTING BACK TO THE SHIP

---

Now I am once again all by myself over unfriendly waters and probably a few hungry sharks. My instinct told me Iwo Jima was in a southwesterly direction. Once again I began a mild climb with moderate speed and with the mixture control as lean as I could get it without sacrificing speed. I needed to fly as lean a mixture as possible because I had no idea how far away the carrier was and I was trying to conserve my fuel, since I had dropped my belly tank a long time ago and with all the high speed maneuvering I was getting low. I had to allow 200-300 miles to go to get back to the ship. Also, I could be in a heck of a pickle if some Zero jumped me at slow speed and without enough altitude to dive away or dog-fight with him.

Finally, I saw some friendlies mixing it up with the enemy. One of our planes had a Tojo (Latest and fastest, then, of the enemy fighters) on his tail and he ended up so shot up he had to fly back to the carrier, roll the plane over, and bail out. He was later picked up. Meanwhile, somebody closer to our guy shot the Tojo down.

Finally, I gestured to one of our planes that I was getting low on fuel and I needed to go back to the carrier, some 200-plus miles away. Another squadron that attacked after we did came by and I went back with them. Of course, I could have flown back by myself, but preferred to have a little company since I didn't know what I might run into on the way.

One of the reasons I think I had less fuel than some of the other planes and needed to go back earlier was due to the fact that I had been doing all that dog-fighting in both engagements at high speed and it just gobbled it up.

In the early days of the war we navigated by what's called "dead reckoning" to and from the carrier. It is not an exact science because you could work with wrong wind, since winds differ at different altitudes and have to be calibrated while flying the plane. The other factors that I mentioned earlier are not set in stone and can vary from the expected number. Also in rough weather it is often hard to hold the plane steady on the headings and altitudes that are needed to get where you desire to go.

There have been lots of stories about pilots miss figuring and going into the drink because they ran out of petrol. Remember we aren't looking for a stationary target because the carrier is always moving and we have to intercept it. In addition the ships, to avoid subs, are always on a zigzag track and this has to be calculated too.

I recall one pilot who missed his rendezvous with the carrier and in the course of looking for it he flew over a merchant ship. Since most ships adhered to radio silence to avoid sub attacks, he tried to signal the ship with Morse code. Apparently he was a bit rusty and that didn't work so he flew over the ship and tried to drop a message in his shoe as to his whereabouts, and missed the whole ship. So then he tried it again with the other shoe and got too low and ended up going in the drink. The ship was able to pick him up, but it was on its way to Panama.

Everybody thought he was a goner for some time, since the ship was not fast and it took a while for them to get to Panama, and with strict radio silence enforced of course nobody, including his family and shipmates, knew he was still alive. In addition this poor guy had only his wet flight suit and no shoes for all that time, though I'm sure somebody lent him clothes.

In the later years of the war we had a homing device called YE/ZB on the tallest mast of the ship. This sent out a signal in each approximately 15- degree quadrant in a different letter, which was changed daily. It was line-of-sight broadcast so that if you didn't pick it up right away you would just climb to altitude and when high enough you could pick up the letter being broadcast in your sector. Then you'd look up your code for the day and take an opposite heading returning to the ship.

Back to me and my returning to the carrier in the Iwo Jima waters. The leader of the group I joined up with did just what I described above to get back to the task force, where I searched out my own ship and landed aboard. I got credit for one and a fraction kills because nobody saw the last two I shot down and I guess they felt sorry for me and gave me a fraction of one for credit. Some crewman said the gun cameras didn't work. Our leading ace confirmed my shooting down the Tony that was shooting him down. I always felt a little cheated, but I could at least claim I was the first American to see Iwo Jima when I flew over it. Now I can't even say that but can only say I was one of the first.

*Rambling Memories*

It was by far the most dangerous enemy stronghold we flew over and they put up a horrific ground defense to our Marines and Soldiers. We lost several of our shipmates in the attack. I pitied the squadron's officer who had to send the letters to the next of kin.

Out of the scuttlebutt (ship's gossip) we heard that the Belleau Wood, a sister carrier in our fleet, left the states with 36 fighter pilots and only returned with two of the original 36. That had to be brutal.

Years later when a friend at a meeting was describing some of my exploits in WWII, my wife really nailed me. She thought he was making me out to be too much of a hero, so when he said I was one of the first Americans to fly over Iwo Jima, she said "yeah, by mistake". That brought the house down. I've said that many times myself, of course, but I'm sure you can imagine how the other wives loved my wife's remark. (Since she is reading this and she is the love of my life and will be forever, I want to keep her on my side.)

One other aside, many years later I was up for Commodore of the Channel Islands Naval Yacht Club. People asked me to tell something about myself. I said well I was born and they said no don't go back that far just tell us what you did in the big war, WWII. So I said well, I was a navy fighter pilot and I flew off an aircraft carrier, shot down planes, sank ships and more or less single-handedly won the war. One of my buddies was in the audience and he wasn't going to let me get away with that. So he hollers out "Hey Doug, those ships and planes-were they theirs or ours". By the way they elected me anyway.

# CHAPTER 28

## MORE ENGAGEMENTS

Its back to the war. The next engagements are very fuzzy in my memory. I remember bombing runs made on enemy installations on Rota Island, Palau Islands, and others. I know on some raids I came back with holes in the plane but then didn't that make it lighter, therefore faster. I probably failed to mention that we hit Saipan, Tinian, and Guam and the Philippines a number of times prior to the invasions. I remember one of our torpedo bombers saying he had seen this big dust cloud on one of the islands and thought it was a tank, so he dropped a bomb on it. Well it turned out to be a bunch of some poor old farmer's cows. So, naturally he got a couple of cows painted on the side of his plane. It was customary for ships sunk and/or planes shot down to be painted on the sides of our planes but he was the only flyer I know of with cows.

The next big engagement was the Philippine Islands. Our CIC people had discovered a lot of ships, mostly freighters but some men-of-war hiding on the western side of the Philippine Islands. Since our fleets were east and north of those ships, in order to attack them we had to fly over in an east to west direction the entire width of the large island of Mindanao. This island is the southernmost big island when you look at the Philippines from a north-to-south perception with Luzon being the uppermost northern island and Leyte being the middle one. It meant flying over enemy territory with enemy fighters coming up to intercept us, since the Japanese occupied the Philippine Islands. We then made bombing runs on the ships and had to fly all the way back with those same fighters intercepting us. It was a long flight at best.

There were two scenes that I still remember about that flight and I can still see in my mind. First, on our way over we spotted a Japanese heavy cruiser hiding in the harbor of one of the islands. I remember Jim Stewart, the high school friend I mentioned earlier, leading a couple of divisions (eight fighter planes) and peeling off in a split-S maneuver and he and the rest with him making individual

*Rambling Memories*

glide bombing runs on the cruiser. We were around 25,000 feet and I saw the murderous AA fire coming up at Jim and his flight from the cruiser way below us. We watched as we flew over him on our way across the island of Mindanao and I was told later back onboard the ship that they made numerous runs until they finally sank the cruiser. Seeing the intensity of the firepower from the Japanese cruiser that our planes were taking on each glide bombing run and knowing they had to hold their run steady in the glide in order to hit the cruiser showed a lot of guts. These weren't planes bombing at 25,000 feet but planes flying in a dive all the way down to just above the water.

Let's get something straight, you don't hit ships which are moving all over by bombing from 15-25,000 feet. The Army Air Corps tried this at Midway and didn't hit a single one, according to Commander Thach and others who were there. The Army Air Corps' claim that they hit some was later debunked. When questioned about the Army Air Corps claim of hitting Japanese ships at Midway, Thach, who had been at Midway after the B17s had made their runs from a high altitude, said there was no evidence when he attacked the Japanese fleet that any of them had been hit previously by the B17s. He said it was flatly not true, especially since all the Japanese ships were traveling at flank speed and had no apparent previous damage. He also debunked the Norden bombsite that the Army Air Corps was so proud of. At the time he stated that no one can hit moving ships like the ones at Midway from 20-25,000 feet. It's hard enough hitting moving ships when glide or dive bombing and pulling out anywhere from 1500 feet to just above the water.

Actually the Norden bomb sight was developed by the Navy and rejected. Thach said he had probably more time kneeling looking through the bombsight than the bombardiers in the B-17s, since he had been the Navy person who tested it. No one disputes its worth for bombing stationary targets, but it is no good on moving ones from high altitudes, which is probably the reason the Navy rejected it.

Back to attacking shipping in the Philippines. After warding off the interceptors on the way across the island we found the ships in hiding and went into bombing runs. We were lucky these ships had nowhere near the firepower to throw up at us like the cruiser. On one of my first runs one of our dive bombers came into my gun sight from my right side while I was in a dive and at a lower altitude and I had to hold off firing for fear of hitting him. I was so paranoid of hitting him with my 50 calibers that to this day I can still see him coming into view in my gun sight. I also had to veer off for fear of colliding with him. Strange what memories you retain after all these years. I only remember making several runs and all of us sank a bunch of ships. So then we went back over the islands putting up with AA fire and I can't remember if any Zeros came up after us. We returned to the fleet and landed on our carrier.

## CHAPTER 29

### GOOSED!

---

On one engagement I made a skip-bombing run on a merchant ship. I don't feel like taking much credit for this because the ship only threw up a small amount of flak, not at all like men-of-war like destroyers, cruisers, battleships and even aircraft carriers. This ship couldn't have had much more than three or four guns trained on me and he didn't hit me. I started my approach probably around 5,000 feet and dove down to just off the water to build up speed. With the throttle full forward I leveled off at about 10 to 20 feet, sprayed the ship with machine gun fire and just before I got to the ship I dropped my 500-lb. bomb and it skipped right into the side of the ship, blowing up on contact. It didn't have a delay fuse in it.

What I didn't know was that the ship was an ammunition ship. It blew sky high and I caught the blast, knocking the tail end of my plane upward, putting the nose downward headed for the water. It was like somebody had given me an enormous goose. I've been told that on bombing runs the bomb arrives at the spot about the same time as the plane, which would account for my catching the effects of the explosion. I survived that explosion and nobody even painted a goose on the side of my plane. When I collected my wits I turned to look back at the ship I had just bombed and it was listing badly indicating it would probably sink. Our fighters at that time were only capable of carrying one 500-lb or was it 1000-lb bomb each so I couldn't drop anymore bombs on it.

# CHAPTER 30

## COMBAT AIR PATROL

We frequently flew CAP (combat air patrols) over and around the fleet or flew out on headings away from the fleet and checked certain sectors for enemy planes who might be flying under our radar and headed into the fleet to bomb our ships. Sometimes it would be a scouting mission where we flew out from the fleet certain distances and then scouted those sectors. These were mostly boring because we seldom saw anything. I remember one CAP when a squadron mate, Hawkins, and I were the CAP over the fleet. With nothing to do except circle the fleet overhead to ward off any enemy planes that showed up we decided to play chicken. Hawkins later became a leader of the Blue Angels and was featured in the Navy's Air Museum in Pensacola, Florida. He was credited with 14 kills and had an article written about him after the war for bailing out of a jet at supersonic speeds and surviving. This was before the development of the current ejection seats that provide more protection to the pilot. Anyway I have to confess, in the game of chicken where we each flew at one another head- on, at the very last minute I gave way first.

# CHAPTER 31

## THE ONE THAT GOT AWAY

I used to have pretty good eyesight, and on one flight over the Philippines of about 12 of our planes just looking for enemy targets (we called it "targets of opportunity"), I spotted about six Vals, the Japs' dive bomber, before anybody else. These are similar to the German Stuka dive bombers, who incidentally patterned their tactics after our U.S. Navy dive bombers, so don't be giving the Germans credit for inventing dive bombing tactics.

The Val had fixed landing gear with a rear gunner and a single 30-mm machine gun located in the rear cockpit. These planes were easy meat for our fighters. I dove down and yelled "Tally Ho" and was just getting lined up to spray the nearest one when one of our pilots scooted in front of me and I couldn't shoot. I could have killed him. Since I spotted them and it turned into a traffic jam trying to get to the real vulnerable Vals with all of our guys trying to shoot them down, there were something like 12 planes reported shot down. I knew there were only six, so the various CIC officers checked with me to verify the kills. It later got squared away except that jerk pilot denied me an easy kill.

# CHAPTER 32

## FORGOTTEN ACTION

I know I've left out a lot of engagements, but because the years have slipped by so fast I just don't remember them all. I went to my old log book and came up with following names of targets with brief mention that I made bombing runs or strafing runs on them at one time or another. Only the log book knows as they are a mystery to me as to what I actually did. They are Manus, Iwo, Palau, Mindanao, Visayas, Negros, Clark Field, Manila, Cullian, and Manila itself as well as Saipan, Tinian, Guam and Rota and others I told about before. I just didn't write down what happened and sometimes I didn't even put down the name of the enemy location in my log book and I know there were more locations. Of course we also made many more strikes than just one on some of the locations in order to totally wipe out enemy resistance.

# CHAPTER 33

## HEADING HOME

About this time we got the word that we were going home. In those days we were usually gone in the combat zone for a year or so. For the next few missions guys were making bombing runs and pulling up at a thousand feet instead of going all the way down to the deck. I had felt that I hadn't had as much combat as some of the other guys so I volunteered to stay with the fleet and transfer to another squadron, but Jim Stewart talked me out of it. Later I thought I might have made a mistake, as our fleet began being attacked by Kamikazes. These planes usually attacked by starting at an altitude of 20,000 feet then going into a dive to pick up speed and head for one of our ships. I felt they might have been easy pickings particularly if I was in a F4U squadron. This because the Corsair is very fast and I felt I might be able to catch them. Of course there was always the possibility I might have been shot down, too.

Actually what the Kamikazes would do would be to approach our ships and pick one out from a long way off and then begin a shallow dive, so as to arrive at one to three thousand feet near the selected ship. They then would head for it in a steep dive, with the idea of plunging their plane into the ship, blowing themselves up while creating considerable damage. The Kamikazes were somewhat vulnerable if our planes were higher than the Kamikazes and close enough to dive down on them from above, shooting them down before they started their dive on to the ship.

Anyway, I can't remember now what Jim said to convince me that I had done enough of my share, but I went home and have been somewhat sorry ever since.

We offloaded from the carrier onto a merchant ship, a troop transport, and headed for the States. It took about 30 days to get to San Francisco where we would go our separate ways. Most of the time coming home our squadron officers and seamen spent in poker games. Everywhere you went on the ship you could hear games going on. Not being much of a gambler I looked around for other things to do to pass this dull time. One of my squadron mates and I found some boxing gloves and went up on the top deck and sparred a little. I think his name was Zimmerman and he had been a halfback at the University of Michigan so he was in a lot better shape than me. He wasn't all that big but very muscular. After a few rounds and being out of shape we quit. I think I can still feel his punches on my ribs.

We made a stop at Pearl Harbor and were given leave to go ashore. A bunch of us got together and went over to this big laundry where all the laundry on the Navy base was processed. We did this because we heard that there were a large bunch of women working there, and having been without even the sight of women for upwards of a year we wanted to see what they looked like again. They must have thought us nuts staring at them the way we did.

Then I remember going with one or two of my buddies to a restaurant and ordering a scrumptious meal I can remember to this day: Corn on the cob, T-bone steak, mashed potatoes and apple pie a-la-mode. Wow was it ever a change from all those months of boring, canned stuff on board ship. Robert Stack, a movie actor, was eating at the table next to us. During the war he taught skeet shooting on one of the Navy bases as a commissioned officer.

Back aboard again, we arrived a few days later in San Francisco (or was it Alameda?) off-loaded from the troop transport and headed home. We were given two weeks leave. My Dad being the great guy he was let me use his car, but most of my buddies were still overseas and I can't really remember what I did during those two weeks.

*I finally got a good conduct medal !*

# CHAPTER 34

## STATESIDE & TRAINING A NEW COMBAT TEAM

After that leave I had orders to report to U.S. Naval Air Station Melbourne, Florida. There I picked up seven new fighter pilots and it was my job to train them in fighter tactics. My memories are very dim. About all I remember was when I was on the ground at the end of a runway with paddles during the day and lighted wands at night acting like an LSO. I was directing my new fighter pilots in how to land the F6F fighter, since they had not flown it before. I was to train them in fighter tactics and we would leave Melbourne when their training was complete and join the fleet in a fighter squadron with me leading them. There were so many bugs as I stood at the end of the runway I had to have a white-hat (enlisted man) fan me to keep them away.

The new guys were taught gunnery runs as I have described previously (low, mid, high, and overhead runs). We spent some time on fighter tactics such as the Thach Weave, also. In later years, since we were no longer inferior in speed to the Jap fighters this tactic kind of died. With the older F4F in the earlier days it was a great self- protection maneuver.

Upon completion at Melbourne we were given orders to go to U.S. Naval Air Station Glenville, Illinois. This base is located on the shores of Lake Michigan. The Navy had taken a couple of large pleasure ships on the lake and converted them into aircraft carriers. I don't know why, but I have the idea in my head they were powered by large paddle wheels but that doesn't seem plausible. Anyway, they originally had superstructure much like the Mississippi river boats. This all had to be leveled to create a flat top for plane landings. Maybe that's why I have the paddle wheel image in my head. Regardless of their propulsion system, they were slow.

I may have already explained that when a plane lands on a carrier deck it has the speed of the larger carriers which is usually 30 knots to minimize the landing speed of the planes. For the smaller carriers their maximum speed is usually about 18 knots. Then add the wind over the deck of around 30 knots so that his relative speed on landing is 60 or 48 knots less than it would be on land. These Lake Michigan converted ships were not very fast and well under 30 knots; so we needed as much wind as possible to make up for their slow speed. So while we were at Glenview we spent most of our time waiting for the wind to pick up to an acceptable speed for carrier qualifications. These new pilots had never landed aboard a carrier and before joining the fleet they had to become carrier qualified. Since I was their leader I would be re-qualifying even though by this time, of course, I had hundreds of landings.

I had one great advantage over the new guys. I could go on liberty every day the wind wasn't strong enough, and they couldn't. So I spent my time, after checking the wind, going on liberty, drinking beer and chasing girls in Chicago. And there were plenty of girls and not that many guys.

When I first got off the train from Melbourne in Chicago I had caught an El to Naval Air Station Glenview. When it made a stop on the way to Glenview four or five pretty young gals got on the car I was in. This was late at night and the entire car was completely empty with your pick of seats. To illustrate what a shortage of guys there was, these young women all sat down next to, in front and in back of me. I thought I had died and gone to Heaven. Is there ever too much of a good thing.

At Glenview, one compulsory test for all pilots, leaders included, was to climb up a cargo net in the base indoor swimming pool to a bar at the top of the domed ceiling. This pool was very large and I think it was about 26 feet up to that bar. This was as near as the Navy could get to simulating jumping off the side of a ship in the event the ship was sinking. It was also a training time to learn how to jump the correct way so that you entered the water safely. We would then turn around and jump off into the pool, being careful to enter the water correctly and not hit a fellow shipmate. Just before I went one of the jumpers did something wrong and the life guards had to go dive under water and rescue him. This didn't instill a lot of confidence in anyone. When I got to the top I felt the foot of the guy ahead of me and it was trembling. He had been there awhile and hadn't got the confidence to jump. I knew what he was doing, hesitating like that, was the worst thing he could possibly do so I just got to the bar turned around and jumped. It's a wonder I didn't hit somebody as there must have been 25 guys doing this.

I was scared the first time, too, but it turned out to be so much fun I got permission to do it again. Although the whole idea was to simulate climbing up and jumping off the carrier it's not too realistic since the ship's hull is about 60 ft. for the smaller carriers and about 80 ft. for the larger carriers to the water line and this was only 26 feet.

Finally the wind increased enough and we flew out to the carrier. I made my eight qualifying landings with "Rogers" all the way around and went below to the wardroom for coffee while waiting for my team to complete theirs. I have to mention I was pretty hung over. While I was there some civilians in suits approached me in the wardroom and it was explained that they were from the labor unions that were striking or considering doing so. The government people had brought them out to see what we were doing because it was considered somewhat dangerous, so that they might reconsider striking and thus hindering the war effort. Apparently they were impressed by what they saw while there, because they called off the strike and the war effort benefited.

We were given orders to proceed to Naval Air Station Alameda and await further orders. After a couple of weeks sitting around we were assigned to join VF11, Fighting Squadron Eleven in Santa Rosa, California.

While there, four or five of us decided we were going to start our own officers' club in the BOQ (Batchelor Officer's Quarters) at Alameda while waiting to be assigned a fighter squadron. We felt the "O" club could use a little competition. So we went out and bought some booze and set up some tables and chairs, and announced we were open for business. Well, since nobody showed up, we all drank our own booze and got wildly drunk and I think got into some fights. I don't actually remember any fights but next day my face was beat up. But then maybe I just ran into a wall or something. I'll never know. Next day we got our orders to fighter squadron 11 and I had to meet the skipper. I don't think I made too good an impression on him with my beat-up face.

# CHAPTER 35

## My Dream Fighter Plane

Due to my seniority I was made engineering officer in charge of overseeing the maintenance of the aircraft in the squadron and it was during this time in my experience that I was introduced to what I considered the finest propeller-driven fighter plane during the war, the F8F Bearcat. It got little or no publicity because it never made it into combat, having been built too late.

It could take off in 250 feet with 25 knots of wind and a rate of climb so high it held the world's climbing record of ten thousand feet even after the jets came out. It was basically a much more streamlined plane, with a bubble canopy, four huge-bladed props and about half the body weight of the F6F while having the same power plant. It was a beautiful plane to look at. I think the closest plane it looks like was the German fighter Focke Wulf 190.

As a matter of fact in 1943 Grumman engineering test pilot Bob Hall was sent to England to test-fly and evaluate a captured German Focke Wulf 190 fighter and he was so impressed that he convinced Roy Grumman that a lighter, streamlined plane like the Focke Wulf was the answer and the F8F Bearcat was born. It had unique characteristics such as no gun chargers. They were all charged on the ground. The wing tips came off at seven or eight G's. It was a beautifully designed plane and easy to handle. The Bearcat was incredibly good at short-field takeoffs. In 25 knots of wind it would be airborne in 250 feet. On August 29, 1989 Lyle Shelton set a world's speed record for propeller driven planes at 528.329 mph in his "Rare Bear", a much-modified Bearcat but still the same old Bearcat, beating the old record by some 29 mph. It had held this record previously in less modified planes too.

The only defect I ever heard of the Bearcat having was some criticism of its ability to hold up under a lot of carrier landings. As an interesting side note, Lt. Bob Davis of the Navy Fighter squadron 18 VF18 reported in a "F8F Bearcat in Action Squadron/Signa" publication while at NAS New Orleans that he "discovered an area used by Army P-51s and we had a field day, every day with them. There wasn't a P-51 there that we couldn't beat in a dogfight…and we did it for four days" was his comment. It's just too bad the F8F didn't make it into combat.

The Reno Air races kind of started all these modifications after the war and they were all modified considerably but still maintained their original shape while adding bigger power plants, more streamlining, and other modifications. This was also true of the Bearcats that set records. Needless to say the Bearcat won more than its share of these races. The Reno Air races that I know about that the Bearcat won were in 1966, 1969, 1970, 1988 and 1989. There could have been more but due to the limited number of Bearcats built in comparison to P51 Mustangs and others there just weren't as many left to race, and on account of the shortage of them they weren't always entered in the races, so they didn't become as well known as the Mustang.

When I was stationed at Naval Air Station Santa Rosa during the end of the war the skipper of the base made a bet with the commanding officer of the neighboring Army Air Corps base that the F8F Bearcat would beat the P38 they had. The two planes lined up and took off. The Bearcat made two runs on the P38 before it ever got off the ground and the P38 had been stripped of much of its gear while the Bearcat was stock. (The P-38 was the twin engine Lockheed Army Air Corps. fighter with the twin booms ending in the tail behind the streamlined cockpit.)

In all fairness, the P51 Mustang deserves to be named as the greatest all- around fighter plane of World War II because in combat it had an enviable record. It was probably faster than all other fighters except the Bearcat, which the Bear proved in its all-time speed record for propeller planes. Also it was no match for the Bearcat in rate of climb or in maneuverability. But If I couldn't fly the Bearcat I'd take the Mustang any day.

There was one combat difference between radial engine planes like the F6F, Army Air Corps P47, Navy F4U, F8F, F4F and the Mustang, and an in-line engine plane. The radial engine planes, according to many authorities, could take a lot more punishment from enemy fire than in-line engine planes and still make it home. The distinguishing feature of the radial engine was that looking at it head on the engine was round in shape; whereas the inline was thin and narrow in appearance somewhat like a car engine. Of course the inline is probably more streamlined because of its shape.

Prior to the Mustang's heavy involvement in the war, I would have to give the British RAF Spitfire the number-one position of wartime fighters, as it appeared to have pretty well bested the Me-109, the German fighter. The two were somewhat similar in speed but the Spitfire was more maneuverable and had a higher rate of climb, so I'm told. The Spitfire's kill ratio in the battle of Britain was much higher than the German fighters produced which was one reason Hitler called off the battle of Britain.

While I was at the Naval Air Station Santa Rosa a ferry pilot brought in a F8F for our squadron. We were slated to board an aircraft carrier in San Francisco with all new F8Fs. I begged the Skipper to let me take up the Bearcat. He okayed and I got into the cockpit, started her up and taxied to the runway. I had read the engineering manuals and other instructions but I wasn't prepared for the acceleration. I shoved the throttle all the way to the wall. It was like a dog on the end of a leash. I went bouncing down the runway straining to get airborne. One of the problems was that in order to eliminate weight, the pilot had to crank the canopy closed and do it at fewer than 180 knots. If I remember, the pilot also had to pick up the wheels and do that under 180 knots. Slamming the throttle all the way forward, I had gone right by 180 knots very quickly and had to slow down to actuate those two functions. Once I was clean (gear and flaps up) and airborne, I just couldn't resist doing an Immelmann, hoping the tower couldn't still see me. An Immelmann is where you go into a loop and roll over at the top. I was pretty low and I caught a little hell over that. I remember the Bearcat required no extra power to do a loop, in fact at the top it had a tendency to still want to climb. It was an incredible climbing machine. The record I mentioned before was established by climbing to 3000 meters (9,842 feet.) in 91.9 seconds.

I flew the Bearcat down low over the Russian River but I was going too fast and just couldn't keep up with the twists and turns of the river. Then I flew over into Yosemite Valley National Park and discovered the Bearcat was just too fast to fly down into the valley and then pull up quickly so as to not run into one of the canyon walls. What an airplane!

Doing that Immelmann reminded me of the time during the war at some point while in the fleet, I did a slow roll right by the ship's island. I caught hell over that as someone thought it was too close to where the captain of the ship sat and might have caused him to spill his coffee.

## CHAPTER 36

### THE END OF THE WAR

I am not sure but I think that the air group I was in at Santa Rosa was Air Group 11. It consisted of a fighter squadron, a dive-bomber squadron and a torpedo squadron. It was scheduled to go aboard one of the big carriers, when all of a sudden we had dropped the big bomb and the war was over. If it hadn't been for the bomb, I would have gone into combat again. I might have bought it and thousands, probably millions more Americans and Japanese would have died as well.

I read later that the Japanese had a complete plan where every Japanese man, woman, and child was given a location were they were to go and provided with anything from pikes to swords and whatever guns that were available, to defend their homeland. They were each given orders not to allow the Americans to put one foot on their homeland. They were to die before they allowed it and knowing from their past history I don't doubt that most would probably do just that. Their hari-kari rituals, the Kamikaze attacks and their strong national pride would tend to support the theory that they would die rather than surrender their land to invaders. It took two nuclear bombs to get them to surrender and then only when the Emperor decreed it, while some of their higher-ranking officers still wanted to fight on. It could have meant the deaths and injuries of millions. My son-in-law's father, who was on a troop transport headed for Japan when the bomb went off, might have bought it. He used to talk about how lucky he had been.

In later years there have been some who said we shouldn't have dropped the bomb because of the horrible effects on the Japanese people. What about the "Rape of Nanking" where many more people than the total casualties from both atom bombs were killed or injured by the Japanese. The Japanese were far guiltier of atrocities than we. Have we forgotten the Bataan Death March, the terrible treatment of prisoners of war and the brutal atrocities committed against the Chinese. Somehow they don't get mentioned in Japan. Dropping the bomb was the right thing to do because it saved many more lives than it took.

The war is now over and I know that according to the title of this book I have reached the end of the subject, but for those who weren't around during those days I would like to describe what it was like through some of my memories after the war.

## CHAPTER 37

### POST-WAR TIMES

My next move was to go home for two weeks' leave and then to the separation center. That is where I encountered the two former high school classmates I mentioned earlier in the book.

After enrolling at USC under the G.I. Bill of Rights, the bill that enabled so many servicemen to get a college education after the war, I put in about a semester and met my current wife of 58 years. She was a member of the Tri Delta sorority and a sorority sister of my sister. My wife often says that because she was an only child, she always wanted a sister and that was the only reason she married me. When I meet young guys about to get married I advise them to make sure before you get married that the young

*Rambling Memories*

bride understands you are the boss and in total control. Then, if the young bride shows up run like hell.

This kind of reminds me of how my wife and I got engaged some 59 years ago. It was kind of funny. My buddy Gilbert was having a New Year's Eve party in 1946 at his home, and another one of my buddies escorted her there, since by then I had gone back in the Navy and was stationed with the Naval unit at White Sands Proving Grounds, New Mexico. I called Gilbert's place at midnight to talk to my girl. In those days there were no cordless phones, but people would sometimes get their phones equipped with long cords so they could move them from one room to another.

There was such a racket, she took the phone into the bathroom off the hall so she could hear. Somebody yelled," Where's Avonne?" Somebody else answered, "I dunno—she was on the phone—I guess now she's on the throne." Then she asked me, "So when are you going to get me that ring?" and that was our romantic engagement and the beginning of our long life together, 58 years to date. We got married a few months later.

As I've said many times as an M.C. at various events, "Its been the most wonderful, exciting, thrilling, and exhilarating 58 years of…her life!" This usually brings down the house and of course is not true as I'm the one who lucked out. She has been the love of my life and she should get a medal for having to put up with me all these years. She is a very beautiful gal who doesn't seem to age. Her mother was the same way. My buddies have often times said, "What's a good looking chick like you doing with that grizzly old goat"?

I've since found out that a lot of guys had wives who made the first move to tie the knot because the guys needed to be pushed. A friend of mine, Karl Henning, who was a funny kind of a guy, really had to be pushed because he moved like a snail on any issue. I remember he had been something of a track star at USC and a football star at Beverly Hills High School. To the day he died he kept his kangaroo leather track shoes under his bed. Every fourth of July we would go over to his house for a pool party and he would jump or dive off his garage roof into the pool, the garage being very close to the pool, with a Roman candle in each hand. It was a very spectacular sight.

After one semester at USC, where I was a pre-med student, intending to take over my dad's practice some day, I had decided I would rather go back into the Navy and requested to transfer from reserve officer to regular officer on active duty. Somewhat surprisingly, I was accepted and soon began my second career as a naval officer. I'm guessing they accepted me because of my combat experience, as I can't think of any other reason.

# CHAPTER 38

## SPACE ROCKETS

I was issued orders to White Sands Proving Ground in New Mexico to the small Navy detachment there. This was where the United States tested rockets prior to Cape Canaveral. I was assigned to the job of Navy Range Officer. My job was to observe the rockets, noting where they landed either from an airplane or with ground crews, and to take reports from the Navy chiefs who monitored the theodolites on the rockets' characteristics in flight. I was selected to this duty because along with being a Naval officer I was also a pilot.

Theodolites are simply telescopes mounted on cameras that display information as to angles, distance, and other information on the object they are following. These instruments were placed all along the borders of the rocket range to monitor the flight of the rocket.

On one occasion a couple of the chiefs who had been monitoring the theodolites came to me to report an unusual occurrence. It seemed that during one rocket firing the theodolites, instead of following the rocket that had been fired followed some other object traveling at an almost impossibly high rate of speed and sometimes just stopping and hovering. I took them into the skipper's office and he pooh-poohed the whole incident. Several years later, imagine my surprise when in a book store I came across a book written by that same skipper titled "Flying Saucers Are Real". Go figure.

White Sands is in an area near Alamogordo, New Mexico, near where the first atom bomb was tested. There was much scientific stuff going on in the local area around the base. It was a really interesting tour of duty. Werner Von Braun, the German scientist who had been in charge at Peenamunde, Germany, of the entire German rocket program; James T. Van Allen, who discovered the Van Allen radiation belt; C.W. Tombaugh, the astronomer who discovered Pluto, and many other scientists of this caliber were at the base.

The rocket range was about 200 miles long and about 20 miles wide, all north of White Sands Proving Ground.

The Navy had its own rockets to fire and the Army had its rockets which for the most part were the German V2s that had done so much damage in London, England. I got a complete tour of the workings of the V-2 and I must say it was remarkably well ahead of other missiles. It even calibrated the rotation of the earth in its guidance system. The Navy's rockets seemed for the most part to be ones built in the U.S. Incidentally the German scientists told us they got much of their knowledge of rockets from the American scientist Robert H. Goddard.

Once The Soviet Union launched their Sputnik we seemed to be trying to develop a rocket powerful enough to compete with them. So the Navy and the Army competed with one another to be the service to win out for this job.

The spotting planes we flew were a B-17 and several little L-5Es (Army spotting planes). Don't ask me why the B17. These were the days after the war and military spending was severely curtailed so we took what we could get. I flew a few times in the B17 and to me it was like driving a big truck and not very practical for this job. The little L5s were really good little spotting planes.

It was an interesting tour of duty and I got to know a lot about the V2, which was an amazing missile for its day.

However sometimes they would blow up on the launch pad, or they would veer off course and go hit somewhere in Mexico, which didn't make us very popular down there. The V-2s made a horrendous sound taking off and could be heard clear into Las Cruces, which was many miles away. For safety reasons we observed them from a blockhouse quite a distance from the launch pad.

# CHAPTER 39
## COMING DOWN TO EARTH

After the war it was almost impossible to buy a car or a house or any household appliances or furnishings because almost all the factories had been busy manufacturing war materials and it took a while for them to tool back up for peacetime items. Some business people took advantage of this.

Before I went back to California to get married and bring my new bride back to Las Cruces, the nearest town to White Sands, I started looking for a place for us live in. After lots of looking and getting desperate with time getting short, I ended up with two choices: a motel or a crummy four-room, cement-block dump in the middle of a potato field on the outskirts of Las Cruces. That was it—there wasn't anything else to rent or buy in the whole city. The motel seemed to be the wrong choice because of its limitations as a long-term home, so I picked the house.

It was about 600 square feet or less and all broken up into tiny little rooms. The living room was about 7ft. by 4 ft. If you had guests you had to talk to them around the corner into the next room that was about the same size. The kitchen and bedroom were not a whole lot bigger. The kitchen sink was just a wooden table with a hole in the middle and a pan stuck in the hole for the basin. Nothing was level including the sink, basin and stove. Little mice and other critters would stick their heads up in the irregular spaces where the floor was supposed to meet the wall.

The house was located on a curve in the road on the outskirts of town. People would slow down at the curve to toss out unwanted puppies and kittens and my wife would take them in and feed them and nurse them along so we always had lots of them to give away. My executive officer, (the exec is the second-in-command of a unit) asked me to find him a puppy. He said they were looking for a small male. Well, my wife came up with this dog that has got to have been the ugliest dog alive at the time. It had small feet, giving us the idea it would be a small dog. It grew up to be an extremely tall dog, though with small feet. It also turned out to be a female. I sure thought my wife knew the difference. All this sure didn't help me when the executive officer got around to writing my next fitness report. Also, pretty soon people from the base started avoiding us when they saw us coming.

The lights in that little shack were bare bulbs turned on by pulling a piece of string. It had a huge oil stove which took up most of the "living room." The stovepipe was just stuck through a piece of board across the top of a window. On one occasion the oil stove blew up, spewing soot all over everything.

I had kept telling my young bride that it was a dump, all the way from Southern California to New Mexico but I don't think I convinced her. I'm afraid she was thinking it was going to be a picturesque little adobe hacienda. I swear her face dropped a mile when we drove up to it and she saw that square, gray, slightly overgrown outhouse for the first time. In addition I paid the landlord $50 under the table to get it. Fifty bucks in those days was a lot of money. His name was LaFitte and I think he was a direct descendent of the pirate. He knew what the rental allowance was for my rank, too, and that's what he charged for the place. I wasn't too cheap to pay more for a house. There simply weren't any others to be had.

*Rambling Memories*

You couldn't get a new car anywhere, and good used ones were almost as hard to find, but my dad had helped me get a used '37 LaSalle coupe from a car dealer he knew in L.A. I was the envy of every white-hat on the base because it went about 70 to 75 miles per hour up the steep Organ Mountain highway between the Navy base and Las Cruces. When I finally sold it a couple years later to a sailor, it had been so hard to get tires or inner tubes that the tires had a bunch of bald spots. So I jacked up the wheels and moved all the tires so the bald spots were on the ground, and wouldn't show when the poor guy came to my house to buy the car. Later, that sailor told me that the tire dealer he took the car to wanted to know if he wanted him to retread the inner tubes instead of the tires, they were so bad. I suppose it was a dirty trick but I did mention to him when he got it that he might want to have the tires looked at.

# CHAPTER 40

## BACK TO THE SEA-GOING NAVY

After a while I looked forward to ending my rotation at White Sands and getting transferred back to the Naval Air Arm. Finally my orders came through to Join VO 1, an observation squadron in San Diego. I had hoped for a fighter squadron, but it wasn't to be. What do they call it, "the needs of the service". Maybe the assignment officer thought I was getting too old, though I was only 26. Who knows?

Before joining VO-1 I was ordered to a training base on the east coast to learn how to handle the single-engine sea planes that were kept on cruisers and battleships in those days. Nowadays, they have been replaced by helicopters. From there I went to VO-1 at North Island Naval Air Station in San Diego and there I was assigned by the squadron to shipboard duty.

I spent a short while on the USS Springfield, a light cruiser, and the USS Iowa, a battleship, to familiarize myself with shipboard operations. Finally I received orders to the ship I was to spend the next two years on as senior aviator in charge of the ship's air detachment. This was the USS Pasadena, a light cruiser. On the Pasadena I had a junior officer and about 20 men in my division. In the Navy there wasn't a whole lot of love lost between us "airedales" and the ship's crew so we pretty much kept to ourselves. Ships officers were known as " black shoe officers" and flyers as "brown shoe officers".

As I mentioned, prior to the Pasadena I spent short terms of duty on the Iowa a new, at that time, large battleship and the U.S.S. Springfield, another light cruiser like the Pasadena.

The Iowa was a sister ship to the Missouri where the official surrender proceedings of the Japanese took place. It was so huge that below the water line there was a long, wide corridor called "Broadway" with all kinds of shops on either side just like a small city.

While on the Iowa I had a couple of humorous incidents as officer of the deck while in port. Some of the ship's officers had told me to beware of the sailors who came from the engineering department to stand watch as messengers, or whatever other duties that were needed, while I was officer of the deck. They said some were apt to do anything to get out of working, and how true that was. One of the sailors would hide in the paint locker whenever it was his watch and I would have to send the Marine on duty to find him. Then when he would finally appear he would start coughing and if I paid no attention to that he would start limping. Some of the junior officers had fallen for his tricks but fortunately I had been warned. He didn't get out of the watch.

Then there was the sailor whose job was to tie the small boats to the boom that was put out on the side of the ship when we came into port. He would tie the small boats OK, but then always fell into the water. We finally figured out that he fell in because after being in the water he was eligible to go down to sick bay, where the doc would give him a little bottle of booze. After the booze stopped he quit falling into the water.

During my earlier assignment to duty on board the USS Springfield I was to learn what would be expected of me on the Pasadena. Since Navy aviators are considered to be naval officers first and aviators second we learned what to do as officer-of-the-deck in port and also while underway. Port duty was fairly simple in that we spent our time on the quarter deck where the ship's personnel came and went on board ship. Many's the time I have watched white hats stagger down the dock only to straighten up when they got to the gangplank leading to boarding the ship. I wouldn't have reported them anyway. In case a high-ranking officer came aboard we had to know about side boys and other requirements, but that was about it.

Now, officer-of-the-deck underway is another story. When qualified you were expected to "con" the ship. This meant you were in charge in the absence of the Captain who might be sleeping, or otherwise not on the bridge. You gave the orders to the helmsman to steer the ship in whatever direction and speed that was proper. Sometimes we would practice bringing the ship along side a dock. We did this at sea, by dropping a buoy overboard, then we would back off a way and try to bring the ship along side it by directing the helmsman, giving him the speed to run the ship and the direction to turn it in. Of course, there are no brakes on a ship. Many's the time I must have missed that buoy by a half a mile.

Another difficult job to learn was running the ship while in formation with other ships. While the ship had a navigator, it was also required that the OD (officer of the deck) be sharp in navigation. The Captain, the executive officer and other senior officers have to be convinced you can run the ship before you are considered qualified as officer-of-the-deck under way. I eventually qualified somehow and we actually never did go aground while I was conning the ship.

Shortly after I reported aboard the Pasadena she got her orders to proceed to China. We flew a small, low-wing observation plane that came out after the war called the SC. It had the same engine as our fighter planes but because the large center pontoon that enabled us to land in the water created considerable drag, the SC was considerably slower. If I remember correctly, it had retractable, small wing-tip pontoons too. It also had detachable wheels for when we were at a landing strip.

While the ship was stationed in Long Beach I used to fly over to Catalina Island and race the speedboats coming out of Avalon on the water. They would keep up for awhile until I would pour the coal to the throttle and then became airborne and leave them far behind. Flying the plane off the water to become airborne was slightly different from taking off from land, as torque pulled the plane's right wing up and left wing down in the early part of the takeoff. You got used to this quickly.

The observation plane I was flying was launched on a short catapult by firing a six-inch shell, which actuated the catapult. We landed in the open sea. Wave action was supposed to be reduced by the ship's making a 360 degree circle and then I would land in the center of that circle. It wasn't perfect and sometimes it got fairly rough, even known to flip a plane. After landing, we taxied up to the stern of the ship onto the sled the ship towed, then reached for the hook on a cable lowered from a crane on the ship and hooked it into the hoisting bolt on the plane. Then the plane was hoisted aboard. Flying and landing a sea plane was a lot of fun, but while its function as a spotting plane had served the Navy well in WWII, its days were numbered. As a matter of fact I flew the last of the SCs to be mothballed to Alameda. Shortly after that helicopters replaced all of them.

## CHAPTER 41

### CHINA WATCH

Before I leave the seaplanes I should tell about my duty on board the Pasadena in China. Shortly after I was assigned to the Pasadena it sailed to Tsingtao on the northern coast of China, just west of the Korean Peninsula. There were approximately 25,000 Marines there and I was told they were there to safeguard America's interests. We were using Tsingtao (incidentally, I believe the Chinese name has now been changed) as a port to transfer supplies to Chiang Kai-shek's Nationalist army. They were fighting the Chinese Communists. While at anchor in the harbor, my plane would be lowered over the side into the water and I would take off to spot the current point the Communists had advanced to. I would relay this to the Admiral so that he could know when to get out with the Marines before the

*Rambling Memories*

Chinese Communists got too close. There really wasn't a whole lot of danger of the Chinese Communists getting too close though, because they didn't want to shut down the wealth of material we were supplying the Nationalists, which was then passed right into the Communists' hands, as they were beating the Nationalists and capturing all their supplies. It was like the Commies had a pipeline to all our supplies.

When I would take off in the harbor and go up to the lines to spot the Communists' newest advances I saw strange sights. It was a weird war, as every now and then all shooting would stop and both sides would drink some tea. I remember seeing these large circles of trenches facing each other with troops in them very much like we've been told it was it was in World War I. I don't remember why the trenches were circular in shape instead of in a straight line. Every time I would fly near them the Communists would start shooting at me and I was beginning to wonder if I was ever going to be somewhere were no one shot at me. There was one thing in my favor; they were lousy shots, so I wasn't in a whole lot of danger.

I remember one incident that sure showed the different between our own and the Chinese cultures at that time. To get to my plane in the harbor I had to go past a sentry post manned by Chinese Nationalist guards. One guard was a little slow in letting me through, so next time I complained mildly to the officer in charge. His answer was, "Do you want me to cut off one of his hands or both". I immediately told him "No I don't want any hands cut off, just tell him to let me through without delay next time!". Whew!

Tsingtao was a city the Germans had built and all the buildings were Gothic in design and beautiful, but there wasn't a single unshattered window in any of them. It was a miserable time for China. Some of its coastline had been under the control of European countries and so much had been left to deteriorate after they pulled out.

When you left the ship to go ashore by way of a shore boat and landed on the dock, young kids would try to sell you something. I remember one boy who wanted $100 for a ring at the water end of the dock. By the time I got to the land end of the dock you could buy it for a pack of cigarettes. You had to be careful because sometimes one kid would try to distract you while another stole your wallet. You needed a clothespin over your nose to kill the stench of the area and you didn't dare eat any of their vegetables as they were all fertilized by human excrement. The results would have made Montezuma's revenge look tame. Their horses were for the most part gaunt and even the seagulls looked skinny.

After several months we left Tsingtao and headed to Shanghai. This was a very interesting city and the most heavily populated city I ever saw. The waterfront where the ships docked was called the Bund. It was an area in which sections of the waterfront were owned by various European countries: Britain, France, and the Dutch, to name a few.

We tied up to the dock at the Bund between some of the other countries' ships. Later our ship's air department played other ships' selected teams in basketball. We clobbered them all very badly with scores like 80 to 2. The French spent most of their time complaining or cheating.

We found most of the other ships when we visited them to be very dirty, especially the Brits'. However we always liked to go on exchange visits in the afternoon to the Brits' ship because they served liquor and had very friendly parties. We were forbidden to have booze on board our ship.

The Bund was where all the docks were and when you left it you could go inland up the Yangtze River or leave Shanghai and head out to the South China Sea. Boys and girls ran in gangs everywhere and they could be pretty vicious on the dock as well in the city. It was a tough life for them, all a matter of survival. We were told stories of people sleeping in the streets during the winter time all piled together for warmth, with those on top freezing to death.

On one occasion we took our sea plane ashore to the main airport to fly it with the wheels on it. In order to clear the trolley lines we had sailors manning long sticks to push up the wires. The sight of the plane going through the streets brought thousands upon thousands of Chinese to grin and watch as we went by. I can still see it in my mind. When we got to the airport we found their repair facilities very crude. I think the most often used tool by the Nationalists Chinese aviation mechanics was a hammer.

We were told that when Shanghai's leaders were given $12,000,000 by the US through the Marshall plan to defend Shanghai from the Communist army, the twelve wealthiest Chinese kept the money and conscripted thousands of coolies to build a wooden fence around the city. Graft was rampant.

In trying to remember the happenings while tied to the dock in Shanghai, I probably sound very disjointed but here goes. It seemed like every noon the Dragon Lady would come by steering her "honey barge" in and around the sampans

*Rambling Memories*

on the river and always going right by our ship, usually at mess time, forcing us to close the portholes. People on shore would line up to earn a few cents for producing the human excrement that filled these barges. The aroma wasn't "essence of roses".

When you looked out onto the Yangtze River there were a never-ending number of sampans (small Chinese boats) with a few Chinese junks (larger boats) mixed in. You could literally walk across the river on the boats and never fall in the water. When we walked down Bubbling Well Road, the Wilshire Boulevard of Shanghai, there were so many people it was almost impossible to drive a car or jeep. I never saw so many people in one city in my life.

I bought a suit from a tailor who came aboard our ship. The material was beautiful English tweed; but he made it with a kind of rounded, no-shoulders and pinched-in waist look that was the Chinese style. I didn't end up wearing it much when I got home. As a thank you for buying several suits from him, a couple of other officers and I were invited to the tailor's home for a real Chinese dinner. After that experience it took me awhile before I could go back to Chinese food in the States. The bird's nest soup was real bird's nest soup, gooey, with twigs, etc. and the sugared beetles were just that.

We finally left China after a visit to Hong Kong, which I found really beautiful and so clean. It was like the States. The British had done a really good job of administering it. The cops were all very tall, husky Sikhs and nobody messed with them.

## CHAPTER 42

### HOME AGAIN

---

We left China after two years and returned to the states. I found out that no one had submitted a fitness report on me because the squadron skipper was in San Diego and had not observed me since I left for China. The skipper of the ship was very happy with my performance but thought the squadron skipper was supposed to file the fitness report on me and as a result of this situation I was later passed over for promotion, because those who made the decision as to who got promoted and who didn't had figured something must have been wrong with my performance because for two years there were no fitness reports. I appealed, to no avail. It didn't help much in those days unless you were a ring-knocker (Naval Academy graduate). I had senior officers like the captain of the USS Pasadena tell me I had run the best aviation department on his ship of any senior aviator he had ever had, but since this was never documented it did me no good. In contrast Naval Academy officers who were hard to find to tell them they had been promoted because nobody knew which bar in town they were in, got promoted.

Later I was transferred to the Navy's All Weather Instrument Flight School as an instructor. The skipper of the school said I had been the best legal officer he had ever had. Navy aviators generally have duties other than flying and mine was as the flight school's Legal Officer.

The school was very large because it taught and fine-tuned the instrument flying skills of all the pilots at that time in the Navy. Instrument flying, of course, is done when there is little or no visibility, due to clouds or storms. All Navy pilots have to be taught to fly only by the instruments in the plane.

Because the school was so large there were a large number of enlisted and officer personnel instructing and attending the school. Naturally, when there are more personnel there are more legal problems, so I was kept busy and I felt the very positive recommendation by the skipper should have meant something. But two years' absence of fitness reports did me in even though it wasn't my fault. It was essentially the fault of the skipper of the VO squadron who could have corresponded with the Pasadena's Captain for a report and didn't because he was too busy covering his behind.

I made a trip to Washington D. C., and I pleaded my case but was unable to get anybody to do anything about it. This was primarily the reason that I got disgusted with Navy bureaucracy. It was also essentially one of the important reasons for my eventual resignation from the regular Navy and transfer to the Naval Reserve.

After duty as an all-weather-flight instructor and legal officer I applied to go back into a fighter squadron again. However, the Navy's Bureau of Naval Personnel, which assigned officers, apparently rejected that idea. Maybe by now I was too old--who knows. Prior duty in a VO squadron and time at sea in a battleship and cruisers hadn't been the sea duty I requested, and I was glad to leave it.

## CHAPTER 43

### ANTI SUBMARINE WARFARE AND KOREA

I got orders back to the carrier Navy and an anti-submarine squadron. Our squadron was ordered to Korea three days after the hostilities there broke out, and our carrier left two days later.

I didn't really get in much combat in Korea. Once or twice the fleet called upon some of us ASW pilots who were familiar with the F4U to volunteer to fly into Korea and help depleted Marine squadrons on bombing runs. I remember most that it was one cold place. We made lots of day and night carrier landings in the South China Sea and near Korea during this time and were kept in readiness in case China officially entered the war, essentially providing protection for the fleet against possible sub attacks.

I have to tell one heroic story about my old hiking buddy, Rodney Sprigg. He was in a jet fighter squadron on a carrier off the coast of Korea. On one flight his wingman was shot down over Korea. Rodney landed his jet fighter alongside his wounded wingman on the ground and pulled him out of his cockpit, somehow stuffed him into his own plane, took off and landed back aboard the ship. Remember Rodney and his wingman, when on the ground, were under heavy fire from North Korean soldiers. While we all tended to look after one another, it was a gutsy and dangerous thing for him to have done.

During the Korean War the city of Kyoto, a beautiful city in Japan that had been spared World War II bombing because the city has great cultural value, was used as a rest and recreation (R&R) place for American servicemen. I got a chance to visit the city and see the all-female opera and other sights. At that time elevated and other types of trains were everywhere. The train cars with the wide white stripe around them were reserved just for Americans and I remember one incident when the only drunken Japanese I ever saw in Japan mistakenly got on our car. At the very next stop Japanese police boarded the car and hauled him away.

The Japanese seemed to realize they had a good deal with MacArthur and his somewhat lenient occupation policies.

On another occasion I discovered that it was a requirement that in order to work as a cleaning lady and other jobs at the bases where we stayed the person had to have been a relative of a dead Kamikaze pilot. At first I was a bit apprehensive about this, wondering if they might be a bit vengeful, but the opposite was the truth. When I left things, including money, laying around the room these Japanese ladies would stack the money by denomination. They treated us like royalty. But I was still a little apprehensive when I got a haircut plus a shave with a straight razor scraping my neck from one of those Kamikaze widows who was the barber!

# CHAPTER 44

## Taps

---

At some point in my career I became Commanding Officer of the aircraft squadron I was in--can't even remember the number of the squadron anymore. I had eventually reached the rank of Commander and was up for Captain. In one of the worst decisions of my life, mainly because I was kind of fed up with some of the bureaucratic unfairness of the Navy, I declined to do one thing requested in considering me for promotion, which was just to submit a current picture of myself. Why would they need a picture to decide if you were qualified to be a Captain or not. If I had been promoted, I would be receiving probably a couple hundred a month more in my retirement pay today if I hadn't been so one-way. Due to my many years on active duty, especially on ships, I probably would have gotten it. So much for would-a, could-a, should-a.

I would like to repeat myself here. Earlier I have said that I wasn't a real hero of the war and that I regarded the Marines and Army guys on the ground along with all those who didn't come back as the heroes. I feel very strongly about this. My war was an impersonal one. We didn't have to fight in hand-to-hand battles in steaming hot, bug-infested jungles rampant with malaria and other diseases, or go straight into the face of machine gun nests like in Normandy and on the Italian shores. We saw no blood and gore except maybe our own. In our case it was either the enemy shot me down or I shot him down. I want to make it clear those guys are the ones who deserved the greatest credit.

The most profound effect of losing a buddy that I had to experience was a vacant seat at the dinner table. Later in the States I got a couple of phone calls from wives whose husbands didn't come back and that could be hard to handle.

When the Iraq war started, I was 83 years old. I applied at a local Navy recruiting office to go back on active duty. I told the recruiting Chief that I understood the Navy was losing a lot of their pilots and that I would be happy to go back on active duty if I could be guaranteed a fighter-pilot billet. He looked me over and told me the Navy wasn't really interested, but I might go check with the Air Force. How insulting can you get?

# Epilogue

Following my retirement in the Navy I went into the Property & Casualty Insurance business and operated my own agency. Some 30 years later having built it into a multi-million-dollar agency, I sold it and retired to God's country, the state of Washington. I live on Camano Island, which is between Whidbey Island and the mainland and south of the San Juan Islands. Very beautiful country which gets about half the rain Seattle gets.

Every now and then I go over to Whidbey Island and attend a lunch or dinner at the Retired Officer's Club. Unfortunately I don't have much in common with many of the other members since we World War II retirees have mostly passed on, dying out, at the last I heard of, at the rate of 1500 per day, maybe more by now. Of course this makes it a little easier to exaggerate a bit with the younger generations, not that I ever would.

THANKS FOR READING MY STORY

Doug McLaughlin

Printed in the United States
65978LVS00005B/196-222